Once Upon
an Island

Once Upon an Island

MATILDA SILVIA

HotHouse
PRESS

Though we have endeavored to confirm the accuracy
of dates, names, and places, the work is essentially from
the memory and notes of Matilda Silvia.

Printed in the United States of America

Library of Congress Cataloging-in-Publication Data

Silvia, Matilda
  Once upon an island / by Matilda Silvia.
    p. cm.
  ISBN 0-9700476-5-7 (hardcover)
  1. Peddocks Island (Mass.) — Social life and customs — 20th century.
  2.Peddocks Island (Mass.) — Social life and customs — 20th century —
  Pictorial works. 3. Silvia, Matilda. 4. Peddocks Island (Mass.)
  — Biography. 5. Bies family.   I. Title.
  F72.P7S55 2003
  974.4'82 — dc21

                                          2003007510

Book design by Melodie Wertelet

Hot House Press
760 Cushing Highway
Cohasset, MA 02025
www.hothousepress.com

DEDICATION

*My thanks to my beloved parents
for their great love and dedication
to our guidance and well being
at times when it was difficult.*

ACKNOWLEDGEMENT

*Leslie and I would like to thank
Don Kupperstein for his friendship and
expert legal advice that helped us to
remain on Peddock's in challenging times.*

Contents

Publisher's Note

The clean up of Boston Harbor has brought a renaissance to the Harbor Islands, which have experienced the passing of time since the prehistoric era. Deposits of soil and granite from glaciers formed the Islands. Native Americans brought their cattle to graze, while Portuguese settlers reaped "fruits of the sea" from their shores. Islands, with names such as Raccoon, Deer, Sheep, and Calf, had history row by them: from the colonists invading the Native American territories during the King Phillips War to submarine nets connecting one island to the mainland to protect the safe harbors from Germans during World War II. Other names such as Moon, Nut, Grape, Slate, Ragged, and Green personify the variety of nature that each island offers. This book celebrates the Islands by tapping into one individual's memory and her family's photo album to bring Peddock's (also spelled Peddocks) Island to life.

Each island claims its own history. George's Island housed prisoners in Fort Warren as early as the Civil War. Boston Light, one of the oldest (still standing) lighthouses in New England, was constructed on Little Brewster Island in 1716. During the early to mid-twentieth century, suspicious harbor visitors were quarantined on Gallop's Island and treated in its hospital. Military forts were positioned on many of the Islands where training and housing occurred. Forts with names like Independence, Strong, Standish, Warren, and Andrews guarded the harbor, while making living for many of the non-military residents quite interesting and challenging. For Matilda Silvia and her family, growing up on Fort Andrews provided exposure to prisoners of war, military maneuverings, and army etiquette. In this memoir, Silvia recalls her, and other families' lives on Peddock's Island.

For over a century, Matilda Silvia's family experienced two world wars, many new inventions, and the every day challenges of living on an island. In 1904, her father, a tailor for the army, arrived on Peddock's when Fort Andrews was first being constructed. Then, in 2001, her daughter, Leslie, had to sell their home to the Metropolitan District Commission (MDC) who had taken ownership of the Island in 1970. With a century of history, Matilda illustrates the strong sense of community that developed on the Island.

When Mrs. Silvia approached me nearly three years ago about getting her manuscript published, I read the half-pencil-scrolled and half-typewriter pages. What came across was her voice, like a stately grandmother telling her grandchildren about a time gone by. But like a grandmother's stories, the chronology of the original manuscript jumped around. However, seeing *Once Upon an Island* for what it was—a celebration of the Boston Harbor Islands—publishing this gem became a must. The only issue was that shortly before our first meeting, Matilda entered the hospital for a routine procedure and tragically encountered a medical complication. As a result her memory was not completely reliable. So, we needed someone who could fill in the missing pieces.

Matilda's extremely busy daughter Leslie responded, having held on to the many stories and facts her mother had told her over the years. Leslie recounted and furnished us with information to augment her mother's manuscript. Thus Sally Weltman, our editorial director, was able to structure and complete the memoir.

As Leslie spoke of her own childhood, one could hear the distinctive voice of Matilda in her daughter's words: "Peddock's was the center of life. Once you lived there, you never wanted to live anywhere else. It was the people who surrounded you that made it like no other place. And when a storm would come, you could only hear the water that engulfed you. This is what set the whole mood."

I would like to thank Matilda and Leslie for handing the stories down to us and entrusting us with over a hundred photographs, that Sally Weltman was able to shape into an historic and heartwarming celebration of life on Peddock's Island in Boston Harbor.

Once Upon
an Island

Construction of an Island Fort

My family's wonderful and unusual life on Peddock's Island began in 1904. My father, Alex Bies was assigned to Fort Andrews, a new army post situated on Peddock's Island in Boston Harbor, just across from Hull, Massachusetts.

In 1889, at the age of eighteen, Dad had come to America from Poland. He settled in Schenectady, New York. He learned to read and write English from other Polish immigrants living there, since there were no classes available to help adult immigrants learn English. Dad also learned tailoring, as he was an apprentice in a Polish owned tailor shop. He augmented his skills through a correspondence course called "Progressive Tailoring" and through its illustrated book.

My father, Alex Bies' arrival in the U.S.

Within a few years, he enlisted as a tailor in the United States Army. He spent about six years at Fort Apache, Arizona. However, in 1898, during the Spanish-American War, he was dispatched to Puerto Rico. He remained there until well after the war was over. His tour of duty was finished, and he reenlisted and was ordered to proceed to New York.

The long ocean voyage from Puerto Rico to his new destination was miserable since it was early March. The soldiers were packed like sardines on the Army transport. The farther north they traveled, the rougher the seas became. Seasickness in cramped quarters does not conjure up a pretty picture, and it seemed that everyone was sick. It was a cold, bleak, windy day when the troopship made its way into New York Harbor and docked on the island home of the great lady with the torch in her hand. Here, at Fort Wood on Bedloes Island, Dad remained for a fortnight until final orders arrived.

His new enlistment destination was Boston, Massachusetts. When he got to Boston, he had seen enough water and hoped his contact with the ocean would be over forever. Little did he know that his new home would be on another island, plunk in the middle of Boston Harbor and that he would spend the next thirty years surrounded by the sea!

When Dad's outfit, the 59th Company Coast Artillery Corps

My father's tailor shop in Fort Apache. He's sitting in the background as his assistant Pepe fits a soldier for civvies.

Dad stands on the shore of his new home during his first few days on Peddock's. Hull Gut and the Fort Andrews' dock are seen in the background.

(CAC), landed at Peddock's Island in early spring 1904, they found very little to be cheerful about. Colonel Vestal was the Commanding Officer (CO), who signed Dad's reenlistment papers and welcomed him to the new Army post that had yet to be built. It would be known as Fort Andrews, named after George Leonard Andrews, a foreign language professor who served as Major General of Volunteers in the Civil War.

On the East Head of Peddock's across from Pemberton, the peninsular point of Hull, Massachusetts, all of the buildings that comprise an Army installation would be constructed: barracks, a hospital, quarters for qualified married personnel, a fire house, bakery, and gym. Lighters (a.k.a. freight barges) were already arriving laden with red brick, cement, and other building materials. Construction was underway. This meant that any of the Portuguese fishermen and early settlers that lived on East Head had to move their cottages to Middle Head, since they were not military personnel. Fortunately, two years before the rumors spread that the Army was coming, several of those

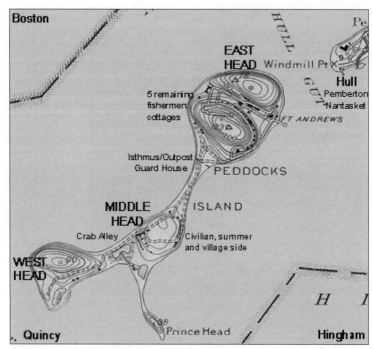

Peddock's Island: When the Army constructed Fort Andrews on East Head, the early settlers and civilians had to move their homes to Middle Head.

homes had already been moved over to Middle Head (which would later be referred to as the civilian, summer, or village side) beyond the Army reservation.

By 1904, the few remaining civilian homes on East Head that would interfere with the installation and those that were ramshackle would be destroyed. Of course, there was one exception. A row of five tiny Portuguese cottages remained on the East Head, on the west shoreline facing Hough's Neck, in Quincy, Massachusetts. Once the civilians vacated these cottages, a few enlisted men and their families, not ranking high enough to live in the quarters would be able to occupy them. The "demarcation" lines between Fort Andrews and the civilian side were very clear on Peddock's Island, with an

MATILDA SILVIA

A view of the civilian side (Middle Head) from Fort Andrews (overlooking Hough's Neck in Quincy) with the outpost/guard house (lower left) separating it from the military side. The Island Inn (center) was notoriously nicknamed the Headache House Hotel.

isthmus and a guarded outpost separating the two sides of the Island.

When the heirs of the Andrew Estate, who owned the entire Island, agreed to lease the East Head to the Federal Government for 99 years, the other side of the Island was considered to be still a part of the Andrew Estate. That meant that the civilians paid taxes to the Town of Hull on behalf of the estate. The Portuguese fishermen, summer residents, and early settlers owned their homes, but paid rent for the land. (This would come into play in the later part of the 20th century, when the Metropolitan District Commission took ownership of the Island.)

During construction, the bulk of the Army lived in huge pyramidal tents—fine in May and the next several months— but terrible in the cruel winter with ice and snow and strong winds. Dad wondered how he would be able to continue his military duties as a tailor by sewing during the frigid cold in a tent that they were supposed to occupy for the better part of a

The army lived in these pyramidal tents during the construction of Fort Andrews.

year. Pepe, a short tailor's apprentice, who Dad had brought with him from Puerto Rico, found New England cold even in May. Unless Father could arrange to buy one of the remaining cottages on the Fort Andrews' side of the Island from a former resident, there would be precious little tailoring done during the coming winter months.

Being a tradesman, Dad was in special service, which meant he performed only certain duties and drills. The rest of the time was devoted to tailoring. Most of the uniforms issued by the quartermaster required individual fitting. Dad received small fees for doing these alterations. Some soldiers preferred drawing a clothing allowance and having their uniforms made. This plus making civilian suits provided my father with a supplement to his some $6 to $8 a month Army pay. But, without the appropriate shop, no new uniforms, no repairs, no cleaning or pressing, and no new civilian clothing to wear when the soldiers left "The Rock" (as the Island was aptly nicknamed) on weekend pass, would not set well with anyone.

The last and best of the old summer cottages remaining on the new fort was owned by Mr. Pope, a Boston lumber dealer.

Dad (far left table, second one in on the right bench) joins the rest of the 59th CAC inside the mess hall tent during construction.

It sat right next to the guard house on the dock, that the Army used for transport and faced Pemberton in Hull. Dad contacted Mr. Pope and made a deal to pay $100 for the house, shed, and all contents with final payment due in July. Now they could have a tailor shop in a well-built cottage. There was plenty of room with both upstairs and down. What's more, it was partially furnished with some nice pieces of old furniture, English china, and oriental bric-a-brac. There were stoves, and after some winterizing they could be comfortable and snug. Also, there was ample room for the cutting tables, ironing boards, cleaning materials, sewing machines, and other tools of the trade. The rooms upstairs would be for sleeping, and they could prepare food in the meagerly equipped kitchen when they wanted a change from Army food. Best of all, it was only a few steps away from the dock and the Army Post now under construction. Expectations improved and enthusiasm for a new kind of experience on a water bound rock took over.

Dad was very pleased with his house purchase since he remembered all too well the cold winters spent as a laborer on the railroad in Schenectady when he was a new immigrant. He

Two soldiers stand in front of the building of the main headquarters circa 1900.

now set up shop, and business quickly became brisk. There were many orders for civilian suits, which made my father especially happy since he had many samples of fine woolens from the Detmer Woolen Company of Boston. Soldiers just up from the tropics wanted suits of warm wool for the cold and to be able to sport them in the big city of Boston.

Busy years slipped by. By 1910, most of the buildings on the fort were built and occupied. Fort Andrews was a beautiful

Some of Dad's "customers" pose with their mascot during the construction of Fort Andrews.

Fort Andrews had all the amenities for the soldiers, including this rec room in the enlisted men's barracks.

Post. The landscape only enhanced the beauty of the architecture. The red brick barracks sat in an impressive, slightly terraced row, bordering one side of the parade grounds with the road running in front of them, and facing the hospital and officers' quarters on a steep double terrace.

The buildings were three and a half stories high with white pillars supporting a second floor verandah. The first floor contained the mess hall, kitchen, noncommissioned officer's rooms, storerooms, a couple of offices, and the latrine.

A lovely wide staircase led to the second floor where there was a day room (recreation room), a couple more noncommissioned officer's rooms, more storerooms, and a dormitory type quarters for the enlisted men. The third floor was much the same as the second floor. The buildings were roomy with large windows for plenty of light. The tents were gone, but the memories of the hardships of living in them were vivid in the minds of the former occupants.

Army boats made trips to Boston three times a day. Twice a week there was a midnight boat. Weekend passes became

Mother's family on the steps of their Salem home. Notice my mother's dress (far left) that she made from her favorite lace.

routine and Dad made many acquaintances in the metro area. He was tall, blonde, and good looking with a military carriage. His talent for making the beautifully tailored civilian suit that he always wore on pass belied the fact that he was a private in the Army. Dad always seemed to have money in his pocket, and his gentle, kind, soft manner made him very popular with the ladies, which he would later prove on one of his visits to Boston where he first saw my mother.

Mother, Matilda Walker, was born in Salem, Massachusetts during the blizzard of 1888. Her father was born in Poland and arrived in America in the middle of the 1880's armed with more than a simple education. Unlike many immigrants, he could read and write and speak English, Polish, German, Russian and Slavic (which came in very handy when he met my Slavic grandmother-to-be). Mother was the only girl of six children and was adored by her five brothers. As a little girl, she took lunch to her father daily at the cotton mill where he was foreman. The weaving and lovely patterns of the cotton yard goods fascinated her.

In those days, the Salem schools prepared children not only in academics, but also in a profession. Mother learned to sew and how to determine the various types of yard goods, which had attracted her at the mill. She loved lace, which was a very important dress decoration of the day. Her interest in lace eventually led her to a job as assistant buyer of lace at the old Shepard Stores in Boston.

Mother and Dad Meet and Marry

It was while Mother was working in Boston, when mutual friends would arrange the "casual meeting" with Dad. She had no inkling Dad was in the Army and he did not tell her. She held a very dim view of the soldiers and sailors who hung around Scollay Square and the Boston Common, and freely voiced her thoughts and disapproval. Dad was always in civvies (civilian clothes) when he saw Mother and was mute about the Army. All Mother knew was that he was a tailor and his shop was near Pemberton.

Mother was very pretty with long, dark, reddish brown hair, small framed and dainty, extremely proper and formal but had warm flashing expressive brown eyes. She made an imme-diate impression on everyone she met, especially the men. Dad was smitten. The inevitable happened. It was love at first sight, and Dad met the family.

The Army secret finally came out, and Mother reluctantly accepted the fact. Her parents proved a different story, how-ever. Seldom do parents approve of the man their only daugh-ter plans to marry, and my grandparents were no exception. The big blow-up resulted in Mother leaving her parents' home in Cliftondale (a section of Saugus) and moving back to Salem to live with her Aunt Franka. Although my parents would eventually wed, despite her parents' disapproval, there was one

Dad's house stood next to Fort Andrews' dock facing east towards Hull before Mother came on the scene and had him move it.

other slight problem before the ceremony and celebration occurred.

Mother's first trip to the Island—that was to be her home for the next twenty-five years—created a pre-nuptial rumpus. Never would she live so close to the barracks at the foot of the parade grounds where my father's house now stood! It was bad enough to be married to a soldier, but never would she live among them! Needless to say, Dad hastily got permission to move the house. But, the only available place was on the other side of the Fort where the five remaining fishermen's cottages stood and were now occupied.

Moving it over land presented many problems. The roads were rough and narrow. There was a hill to climb and descend.

To take it down stick by stick and rebuild it presented as much difficulty, and time was of the essence. The only way left was to move it by water. Dad was confronted with the Herculean task of floating the house a half mile around the Island on a raft. His future marriage depended on it! His bride-to-be was adamant. Yes, it was going to be a hard job, especially for an Army tailor who originally hailed from inland Poland.

Imagination, ingenuity and common sense proved to be the solution. He would ask permission for the use of the Army tugs to tow it around the East Head of the Island. By Jove, that would do it! He would make a raft and tie buoyant empty barrels beneath it. Enough of them would float the raft and the house. After some calculation, the decided number of barrels were procured and the task of accomplishing the project was begun. Huge 12 foot logs were bolted together to form a raft and the barrels were lashed to the frame. That was the easy part. Dad managed that pretty much on his own. Jacking up the house and moving it onto the raft, however, required additional manpower.

Kibitzers were plentiful with many suggestions and wisecracks but nothing constructive. Until permission could be obtained to enlist the aid of the current bunch of inmates of the guardhouse, little could be done. The prisoners arrived on the

One of the empty barrels that Dad used to float his house around the East Head of Peddock's.

In July 1910, two men jacked the house in preparation for its trip over the open seas. The house literally sat in front of the headquarters building and on the parade grounds, from which Mother insisted the house be moved.

scene and tried to move the house. It was then that pandemonium broke loose. Some men manned jacks, others manned rollers, and others manned the hawsers to drag the house onto the raft. Dad gave the commands and masterminded the job. The house started to roll. It rolled so far and fast it slid off the raft. It dredged up the sand and the rocks, and refused to cooperate. The only solution was to dig it out, jack it up again, and slide it back to where it belonged.

After a couple of days and many hours of back-breaking work, digging and jacking, the house was ready to float. Cheers went up and the Army tugboats, *Bumpus* and *Goldbrick*, picked up the hawsers and began the trip around the Island. Everything was going great guns! The house was riding high, and it was almost around the Island to the point where it was to be beached on the far side of the hill to the west of the Post. Dad was happy and very pleased. The mission was practically accomplished.

Suddenly, without warning, barrels started flying skyward and ropes flew like strings of cooked spaghetti. The house was

The floating of the house!

slowly sinking in about twenty feet of water! Dad, usually calm
and methodical, became frantic. Shouting orders to everyone,
he jumped over the gunwales onto the raft. The fact that he
could not swim never entered his mind. Up to his waist in the
water he secured another hawser to the nearest rafter and
threw a line to the tug. The deckhands secured the line around
the capstan and the smaller tug pulled the wayward house

TUGS TOWING SHIPWRECKED HOUSE
AROUND SANDY PEDDOCK'S ISLAND

DISASTER MET IN VOYAGE OF ISLAND HOUSE

Looking like some new type of warship, the house of Alexander Bees of Peddock's island made a disastrous trip around the island today.

It lost its chimney overboard, but was finally triumphantly beached by the tugs Bumpus and Gold Brick on the opposite side of the island from the start after some exciting man-euvreing. The only casualties on the trip were those suffered by two rats, who were tossed overboard as the house wabbled through the waves.

Bees is a tailor and makes government uniforms. He wanted to move his house but couldn't see how he could get it over the Peddock hills. Some of the privates of the harbor forts therefore thought it would be a fine thing to move the house by water. They got 150 oil barrels, mounted the house on a skid and tied and nailed the structure onto a box raft erected on the barrels.

The good tugs Bumpus and Gold Brick were pressed into service and started to pull the house-boat round the island. The start was good. The house moved majestically and then—Bing!

Barrel after barrel got away from its moorings and leaped up into the air as if shot from a mammoth gun. Private Bees stood on land pulling his hair and shouting. The house went down sideways in the water and its blinds were partially torn off.

The chimney then went overboard and sunk. At last the house was beached on the Boston side of the island. The harbor was filled with oil barrels.

Private Bees doesn't think much of moving a house by water.

September 10, 1910 article about my parents' woes for what would be such a simple task a century later.

It made it with a few windows still in tact, but no chimney!

close to the beach. Dad came ashore drenched. He started shivering uncontrollably. The cool September air set off an attack of chills and fever, a residual of the malaria he had contracted in the tropics (these attacks were to recur for the rest of his life). His assistant, Pepe, got dry clothes for him, and someone produced a cup of hot tea. So much for this accomplishment.

Now a new challenge began. Drag the house from the beach, up the slope of the hill 50 yards to where it was to sit. The raft was still in good shape in spite of the ordeal. The rollers and jacks came into play again. When everything was prepared and secured, the skinner arrived with the mules. They were hitched in tandem and attached to the raft. Army mules were stubborn and downright ornery, but after some gentle and not quite so gentle persuasion, they slowly but surely pulled the house to its final resting-place.

There was no cement foundation or cellar, just a small ex-

Our home joined the five remaining Portuguese lobstermen cottages on the west shore of the Fort Andrews side overlooking Boston.

cavation in the earth for a hollowed-out crawl space about five and a half feet deep. The house was set up on brick and granite blocks just high enough for air to circulate. If a permanent foundation were built and the house fixed to it, the dwelling would become Army property. If unattached, it remained Dad's personal property.

Now there were six houses in the row. September drew on. Once the house dried out, work began on the remodeling. Sheds were built: one for a tailor shop, another for uniform storage, a wood shed, coal boxes, and a boat and workshop. Mother had made several trips to the Island accompanied by one or another of her brothers, and by the end of October the house was habitable. Water was piped in from Quincy through a water main that had been installed in 1907. At this time, the Army piped water to the cottages occupied by Army person-nel. A new sink and set tub of the latest soapstone were in-stalled. A new kitchen stove, a Glenwood for cooking and baking, was also installed. Wallpapering and painting were done. The house was wired for the new electricity—no more oil lamps. However, there was still much to do to please Mother, but that would come later.

On November 23, 1910, Mother and Dad were married in

Alex Bies with his soon to be wife, Matilda Walker.

a Polish church in Salem. Mother wore a beautiful rust-colored silk suit and ostrich plumed hat that she sewed herself. (Many years later the outfit was donated to the Boston Ballet.) A reception was held at her Aunt Franka's house. There was delectable food and several kinds of homemade wines. Franka was an excellent cook and loved to practice her skills, especially for a gala occasion. The wedding was a small affair

> Mr. Alexander Pies
> and
> Miss Matilda Walker
> announce their marriage
> on Wednesday November the twenty third
> nineteen hundred and ten
> Salem,   Massachusetts
>
>
> At Home
> after December the twentieth
> Fort Andrews, Boston

with close family and friends. A strained peace had been
made with Mother's parents, and they extended good wishes
and joined in the celebration. Mother sent announcements
of her marriage to friends and acquaintances and stated that
she would be making a home at Fort Andrews after December
10, 1910. Where they went on their honeymoon I never
knew, but by the first of the year they began life together on
"The Rock."

Early Island Living

In the early days of marriage, island living was not Mother's cup of tea. She was used to city life and its activity. Most of the day Dad was up in the inner fort at the 59th Co. where his tailor shop was moved and remained until the sheds near the house were built. This left Mother by herself and she was lonely as she had not yet either met her neighbors or made friends. True, she had little free time as there was a great deal of work to do to make the house a home. Hours were spent making curtains for the many windows; the dining and living room had to have drapes. There were the household chores of washing, ironing, cooking, and cleaning to be done. However, the feeling of isolation still prevailed, and for a while tears slowly trailed down her cheeks. Only her great love for Dad and his adoration of her kept her spirits up. There were soldiers helping Dad build the sheds near the house. However, in 1910 on an Army post, ladies needed to be very careful in the way they conversed with the soldiers, not wanting to give the wrong impression. Besides, Mother still did not feel comfortable around soldiers.

The house was in a lovely location looking across the water to the Quincy mainland, the two hummocks of Peddock's Island making a semicircle of land on the south and southeast side nestling a lovely cove to its bosom. Some days, even in winter, the wind was placid and calm. However, at that time of

Mother and Dad worked through the winter to make their newly situated house into a home.

year, a cold cutting northwest wind often blew viciously, making the sea boil wildly. Salt-water spray would spew all over that side of the Island. During these days, Mother loved to bundle up and take the few steps to the beach to watch the tempest and see the seagulls flying low over the water screaming and crying while looking for food in the angry sea.

One day, Mother was sitting on a log tossed up by a wave that Dad had rescued for firewood, when a lady greeted her in rather labored English. It was her next door neighbor, Mrs. Harvey. She had seen Mother but was shy and afraid to intrude. But now was a good time to say "hello." The lady and her husband were from Puerto Rico and were also new to Fort Andrews. Dad did not know them. Though her English was halting, she and Mother understood one another and became good friends and neighbors, each helping the other with small chores like hanging clothes. They exchanged special foods and goodies but never infringed on each other's privacy.

Every week most of the housewives took the long boat trip into Boston to buy meat, fruit, and, particularly in winter, any fresh vegetables the market had to offer. Most supplies were purchased at the commissary, which was around the hill in the huge Quartermaster warehouse. Once or twice a week in the morning, Mother would walk to the commissary to place her order. A teamster in a connastoga-type wagon would deliver it, sometime that afternoon.

When the weather was good, this was a pleasant task. But when winter winds blew and heavy snow fell, it took all of one's strength and stamina to get through the drifted snow. The main roads were plowed constantly during a storm by two Army mules hitched to a weighted iron-clad wooden triangular plow which they dragged behind. The lesser roads and paths were left to each one's own desire and ability to trudge. The biting cold and slashing wind was often worse than the snow. There was almost no place in the lee, and by the time one reached their destination, the cold had penetrated to the bone. Mother suffered frostbite in the little finger of her left hand. After that, when her hands were cold, that finger turned paper white and numb until it was warmed again. She quickly learned that island living presented many hazards to guard against.

Days passed much more quickly than Mother had expected and she met more and more people, including all of her neighbors. Dad and Pepe were very busy in the shop and constantly in need of tailoring supplies, so she was pressed into service to do the buying. Sometimes she would make two or three trips a week to Boston. They took all day—up on the eight a.m. boat, back on the 3:30 p.m. boat that returned to the Island about five p.m.—just in time for retreat. She met many of the ladies from the other island forts on the boats during these trips. They all knew she was the bride from Fort Andrews and welcomed her to the Harbor, where news traveled fast.

Mother's brothers became weekend visitors and relieved

Dad of many chores. They kept the wood-shed full of wood in all shapes and sizes that had floated up on the beach. The wood was sawed by hand to the proper length, split and piled in our woodshed. This pleased Dad, as wood chopping didn't exactly thrill him. My Uncle Billy was a stone mason so he set to work making a root cellar, a front walk, and took care of rebuilding and repairing the chimney.

Mother's aunt and cousin enjoyed the Army boat trips, and visiting an Army post was so fascinating to them that they came as often as they could. Finally, Mother's mother, my "Grand Dame" grandmother, ar-rived to survey the scene. She received, as she demanded, great respect and got royal service from the Army. After a couple of Grandma's well-directed questions upon her first arrival at the fort, the Provost Sergeant

Feeling more at home, Mother knew the protocol and informed Uncle Henry by post how to present himself when he arrived.

spoke to the officer of the day and he dispatched the "Officers" wagon to convey Grandmother to Mother's home. This was the mule-drawn wagon that performed the services of a taxi, but was available only to the officers. If you understood the protocol of the day and the caste system of the old Army, you would realize that this was most unusual. The line between en-listed men and officers was very clearly drawn and that which was reserved for the commissioned officer — including his fam-ily and friends — was almost never available to the non-com-missioned officer, nor his family and friends, let alone the en-listed men. As a result, Mother almost had a heart attack when Grandmother, in wagon, arrived at the front door and the driver assisted her to alight. First of all, Mother hadn't ex-pected her mother and here she was in the officer's wagon!

The Officer's Wagon, a mule-drawn carriage that escorted my "Grand Dame"
Grandmother to my parents new home.

Had her mother infringed on some Army rule and was she "in custody" so to speak?

Grandmother smiled and thanked the driver as Mother opened the door to rescue her. It was Mother who needed to be rescued. Grandmother was a very impressive "grand lady" and handled matters excellently on her own. Her responsibilities of interpreting in the Salem courts had taught her much in the way of handling people, and she treated the young Army men beautifully. They greeted one another with a hug, as Mother struggled to recover her equilibrium.

Grandmother said she had wanted to surprise my mother, which was an understatement. The trip down the harbor, stopping at all the forts, the loading and unloading of freight, the polite deportment of the men, the assistance and kind treatment she received impressed her very favorably. It had not been what she had expected. Her picture of Army life was as Mother's had been, "tough and rough." True, the place was a bit "God forsaken," hard to get to and cold and windy, but once you got there, it was pretty, neat, and apparently alive with friendly activity. Her attitude toward Mother and Dad

Mother settled into island living with chores including landscaping.

softened, and she stayed several days longer than she had originally planned.

Mother was no longer lonesome. Her shopping trips to Boston for sewing supplies for Dad and for home supplies, housekeeping, visiting relatives and friends, helping Dad with various chores, chats with neighbors over the back fence, and special activities at the Post made the time fly. Spring was arriving, and there was a garden to plant and landscaping to do. Several loads of topsoil from the hill were dumped on what was to be the lawn. The climbing rose bushes had arrived and were to be planted around the front and side of the house in hope that they would eventually screen the front porch. A peach tree was planted to one side of the front walk, though I never knew it to produce a peach.

The soil on all of the hills was very rich even though a foot had been removed by the Army and used in other parts of the Post. Each of the companies had their own hill gardens. They grew tomatoes, carrots, beets, cabbage, corn, squash, and beans. The progeny of the asparagus field may still be found scattered around the hills and roads, especially on the south and southeast side of the Island.

The families also had an area they could plant that the Army had plowed with a mule drawn plow. The hill directly in back of the six cottages was for the owners' use, and many, including Mother and Dad, had a good-sized garden and grew practically the same assortment of vegetables as the Army did, only on a smaller scale. There was also an Army orchard with apples, pears and cherry trees, some of which are still in evidence. Gardening on the hill was almost a social event, as each evening after retreat and "chow," families gathered to weed, hoe, and water their plots and, naturally, to exchange gossip, explore rumors, and discuss events of the day. Army kids always had chores, though often it was more trouble for the parents to see that they were carried out than the good they accomplished. I remember weeding as one of the chores.

Summer arrived and brought with it much company. Relatives and friends came on every other boat. Not only did they enjoy themselves, but they also were very helpful. The visitors enjoyed Mother's specially built round bottom rowboat, a gift from Dad. They loved to row around the cove. Those who fished kept us well supplied with fresh flounder, cod, and other bottom fish depending on the season of the year. Mother was very happy and began to enjoy life on an Army post. She also realized that most soldiers were not at all like those she had seen in Scollay Square or on the Boston Common. As a result, her respect grew as she met more of Dad's friends.

Mother also started a sewing circle. The ladies met in the late morning after their housework was done. They had lunch and tea and sewed. She had always made all of her own clothes and most of her mother's. She sewed like a pro and taught the ladies sewing tricks to save time and money—Army pay being what it was. Officers' wives noted her lovely clothes and frequent changes of wardrobe and learned of her sewing skills.

Grandmother Walker on another visit to the Island.

From then on, she was constantly refusing officers' pleas for her to make clothes for their wives. She had little time with all of her activities. Besides, it could also have been an Army version of political suicide for Dad. It was impossible to please them all, so it was best to please no one.

With the coming of fall, it was time to make jams, jellies, as well as preserve vegetables from the garden. There were plenty of berry patches throughout the East Head of the Island. On the rise of the hill in back of the first set of brick quarters on the Post, there were luscious sweet red strawberries. There was another big patch past the incinerator and searchlight battery near the old flagpole — a bit of a walk from the house, but well worth it. Also, Grandmother was now a frequent visitor and brought fruit from her own trees. They both cooked and jarred for days, resulting in a winter's supply of jam, jelly, piccalilli, chili sauce, relishes, vegetables and fruits.

After the first freeze, Dad arranged with the stable sergeant for several cartloads of horse manure mixed with straw to be delivered. He made burlap bag sausages filled with dried eel-grass and packed them around the base of the house, several deep, pushing them under the house. Dad collected the burlap bags for the sausages from the 100-pound potatoes or "spuds" bags that the barracks were only too happy to dispose of. Next came the horse manure, which was spread over the sausages fairly close to the house and all over the gardens and lawns. This procedure helped to keep the floors in the house warm and wind free and at the same time fertilized the whole area.

During the summer he would harvest the long eelgrass which grew in great long patches along the shore. This grass made rowing very difficult at low tide, as the oars caught in the long tough blades that lay very thick on the top of the water at low tide. One could drown if caught in the grass while swimming and no help was close by. After the harvest of the eel-grass, it was dried in the summer sun and then put into the burlap casings. This made perfect insulation as it did not burn and was slow to disintegrate.

With winter, the interminable northwest winds arrived to chill everyone, but the house was snug and warm. Now there were three stoves: one in the kitchen, one in the living room, and one in the upstairs den. There was plenty of wood in the woodshed, and the coal boxes had been built and filled. Dump-carts pulled by mules and manned by military prisoners delivered three or four tons of hard stove coal. The prisoners wore fatigues with a big "P" on the back of their jumpers and an armed sentry walking from behind followed the cart. The prisoners were jailed mostly for being AWOL (absent without leave) or for insubordination. The mules were typical and had to be persuaded with a 2x4 across the rump to make them move. Mother always made sure the mules had a couple of carrots and the prisoners and sentry had coffee and some of her well-liked homemade doughnuts.

Holidays on the Post

T hanksgiving was the first big social event of the new winter season and all of the families were invited to the barracks for dinner. The mess Sergeant of each company outdid
himself. There were tablecloths, quite different from the usual
bare wood tables, flower centerpieces, and white cloth nap-
kins. A printed menu showed that turkey with all the fixings
would be served. It would be the first time Mother would be in
the barracks. It wasn't a place the ladies went unless it was for a

*Families on the Post spent holidays together, one of the few times women were
allowed in the barracks.*

Sgt. Sam Perry (lower left) installing guns.

party or dinner. Everyone had tons of food. The women thoroughly enjoyed not having to prepare a huge holiday dinner for their families. On most local Army posts, a family's closeness and concern for each other was established, especially on the smaller posts, such as Andrews. Therefore, helping each other and spending holidays together came naturally.

Busy weeks followed with everyone getting ready for the Christmas holidays. Mother and Dad were going to Grandmother's for the week from Christmas to New Year's. So, there was much to do making Christmas presents and special holiday treats. Mother made fruitcakes and cookies along with jams and jellies to give to her neighbors.

Among other things, she knitted a stocking cap for Sam

and Consuelo Perry's son, Bill Perry, and a rag doll for their daughter, Viola. Sergeant Sam Perry had been in Dad's outfit in Puerto Rico, where he had met his wife, Consuelo. Consuelo had been a cook and maid for one of the officers on the Puerto Rican post. Her first meeting with Sam was in Dad's tailor shop when she came to pick up her employer's uniform.

There was a brief romance, which was interrupted suddenly when her employer and family were sent from Puerto Rico to a post in Georgia and took Consuelo along. Shortly thereafter, Sam was transferred to Fort Andrews and they lost track of each other. Apparently they were destined for one another, because less than a year later the captain and his family arrived at—of all places—Fort Andrews with Consuelo.

Sam and Connie, as he called her, were married soon after her arrival and he rented the first cottage in the row of former Portuguese cottages, where my parents' house had been moved. A year later their son Bill was born prematurely at home on the Island. He was not expected to live, and needed to be carried on a warmed pillow because he was too delicate to handle. It was touch and go for a few months. Then Bill started to gain weight, which he never lost! His sister, Viola, or "Vi" was born a couple of years later. Connie worked for several officers up "the line," which was the row of officer quarters along the inner fort terrace. She scrubbed laundry on a washboard, cooked, cleaned, and did anything she could to earn $6.00 a week which was the going rate at that time.

Her children, Bill and Vi, usually went with their mother, and on the nice days they were tied outside on a long rope so they couldn't wander away or get into mischief. Connie would keep her eye on them as she did her work, sometimes having to watch her employer's children at the same time.

On Christmas Day, Connie would be very busy the whole day cooking and serving dinner. Her neighbors, including

Vi Perry (left) with a neighbor at Christmas time.

Mother, would see that Vi and Bill were taken care of. Their father, Sam, on the other hand, did not pay much attention to the kids. He was up at the barracks or at the quartermaster's warehouse shooting pool.

When the holidays were over, Dad and his "Doll," as he called Mother, returned to the Island after a pleasant week with her brothers, old friends, and her parents. Mother was Grandfather's favorite, but he still was only politely friendly with Dad. Whatever else, both Dad and Grandfather were gentlemen. My parents were glad to be back on the Island. Besides, Mother had a secret that was only now beginning to show.

Mother began to curtail her activities, staying close to home. She wasn't making trips to Boston for Dad as he now had the new shop next to the house and he could store material, as he needed them. Since telephones were not yet in the quarters, the neighbors kindly took Mother's meat order to the Allen Supply Co. in Boston's North End. The order would be delivered on the afternoon Army boat and then to our back door.

Vi and Bill Perry standing next to their father's chicken coop.

Mother was busy sewing everything for the new baby with yards of lace and embroidery on everything. As I look at some of our baby clothes, handed down from one to another and saved these many years, I wonder how she accomplished such beautiful work. I marvel at the love, patience, and happiness she must have felt, reflected in those clothes.

My brother, Stanley was born in the Homeopathic Hospital in Boston on May 12, 1912, after a seemingly never-ending boat trip from the Island. Mother and Dad were overjoyed with their blond son. Grandmother was proud of her grandson, and he remained her favorite among the three of us until she died at age 93.

When Mother returned to the Island with Stanley, the neighbors offered their help but Mother was quite capable and took the scrubbing and boiling of scads of diapers and baby clothes and all the rest in stride. Dad, not quite comfortable around the new baby and at times slow in the kitchen, helped Mother as much and as often as he could. He even managed to

Stan in his fish box playpen.

do some of his tailoring at home, so he could be nearby. Pepe was always there when he was needed. He often helped Mother lift the huge copper clothes boiler from the top of the cook stove to a stool in front of the soapstone set tubs. She would then lift the boiling clothes from the boiler with a clothes stick and douse them in cold water. After that, the clothes were ground through the hand wringer which was clamped between the two set tubs into bluing water, then through the wringer again into a clothes basket and then out to the line. The ironing was done by heating flat irons on top the stove — maybe six at a time. When they were so hot that a wet finger sizzled, it was time to iron.

Grandmother came often to help care for Stanley, and, of course, one or two of mother's brothers were there almost every weekend. The salt air agreed with Stanley and he grew rapidly. By the next summer, he was toddling around. Stanley's playpen was a big wooden fish box, which had drifted onto the beach. It was cleaned and deodorized, of course, and placed in the fenced-in yard. That was where he would spend many of the good days in the fresh air, while Mother kept her eye on him from the window.

Sometimes in the afternoon the girl next door, Margaret Austin, would come to play. Other times, when Stanley was older, Mother would take them both down the road for a walk to see Sgt. Sam Perry's chickens. Sam had a small flock that once were cooped on the hill, but he moved them down near his house after Claude-Graham White made his historic airplane flight on September 3, 1910, from Squantum Naval Air Base to Boston Light and back. Historic flight or not, Sam would furiously recount how "the damn plane made so much noise and came so close to the hill it frightened the chickens. Chickens flew in all directions, squawking bloody murder and hid in the bush. They didn't come back for days and didn't lay an egg for damn near two weeks."

When the time came for Stan to go to school, he joined the other kids from inside the Post. Each morning they went to the dock at 7:15 to take the Army boat across the bay to The Village School in Hull. A difficult experience at best, and one that I would confront some years later.

World War I

In 1916, Dad's Army routine took some very abrupt turns. Europe was embroiled in a fierce war, and it looked like the United States was about to jump in with both feet. Mortars and artillery were badly needed at various places overseas, so every available weapon had to be shipped to a war area, including the weapons at Fort Andrews. Dad was one of the men called upon to help get the weaponry ready for shipment. While it may seem strange for a tailor to be called in to

Young men lined up to enter the service for World War I.

Soldiers stand in formation in front of the enlisted men's barracks.

dismantle and ship heavy artillery, Dad was an unusually intelligent, versatile, and capable man, and seemingly could do almost anything. Dad, too old for combat, made his mark helping to get the mortars on a barge and eventually off to some war area.

Sam Perry was younger, and he and others from Andrews saw service in France. Connie and his children stayed on the Island and awaited his return when it was over.

My father would be retiring as a First Sergeant in about a year after nearly thirty years of service, which was the accepted number of years for retirement from the Army. Dad had had a couple of years in the tropics, which qualified him for double time—that is two years for one—but he elected to stay in until October 1918 because our country was at war. During that extra year, Dad went daily to Fort Strong on Long Island in Boston Harbor to teach a tailoring course in the Army vocational school, while Pepe took care of Dad's tailor shop on the Post. My father was proud to teach young men how to sew and continue his duty during World War I.

Amidst all of the turmoil of World War I, I arrived on the scene on October 23, 1917. I'm not sure just exactly where I was born. The story goes that Mother was on her way to the hospital. However, the boat was very late and I was very early. So, she didn't quite make it. I arrived on the government boat, as the army boat was called, somewhere between Fort Andrews and Boston—at sea, so to speak. I was never told anything about my birth out of embarrassment, I guess. One did not discuss such personal affairs. I had only heard about my arrival in Boston Harbor from the other Perrys (not to be confused with Consuelo and Sam), who lived next door to us.

Fred and Lil "Nana" Perry had originally come to Fort Andrews from Fort Warren on George's Island. Fred was a handsome American Indian, born in New Hampshire. His wife, Lil, was born at Fort Riley, Kansas Territory. Her father was in the Army and was stationed at Fort Warren where they met. When they settled on Peddock's, Fred and Nana Perry lived in brick quarters on the hill at Fort Andrews for a while. When the house next door to us was for sale, Fred bought it, and became our new neighbor. Nana and Fred Perry told me this story about my birth long after my parents' death.

Stanley was apparently delighted to have a baby sister. As a result, he was a devoted brother to me all his life. He took an active part in caring for me. Though he was only five, he was allowed to give me my water bottle and to rock me in the big rocking chair as well as push me in the wicker baby carriage.

Stan still had plenty of time to play with his friends. He and his friends would do simple things like collect wood, clean up the boat, dig worms by the big rock, or go fishing in front of the house just a few yards from the beach. Being too young, I was rarely invited to go along!

One of his friends, Harry Downes, who lived next door (and later would have the Brookline High athletic field named after him), had a bulldog who didn't get along very well with our terrier, Spike. The two dogs were often at one another's throat. This canine war sometimes put a mild strain on the

From left to right: Me, Stan and our cousin on one of Stan's adventures.

friendship. However, the friendship survived until several years later when Harry's father, Sergeant Downes, retired and moved away with his family.

Spike was devoted to Stanley. When Stan went rowing in the skiff, Spike was the back seat passenger. Every time Stan rode his bike, Spike ran alongside; and a walk on the beach found Spike exploring the flotsam and jetsam, too. They were together the day we almost lost Stan. In 1919, erosion began to make its mark forming pools of quicksand at the base of the steep hill which faced Hull Gut. Stan, then only seven, often walked the beach with Spike. One day he unsuspectingly stepped into a bed of quicksand. He started to sink, and despite his frantic efforts to free himself, he sank deeper and deeper.

Like many animals with their uncanny sense of impending trouble, Spike sensed Stan needed help. The little dog took off hell-bent for home barking frantically. He reached Dad in the shed, grabbed him by a fatigue pant leg and was desperately tugging, pulling, and dragging him in the direction of the disaster. Dad, realizing Spike's actions were very unusual, knew something was wrong. He ran after Spike and got to where Stan was sinking in the sand, now up to his armpits. With a rig of planks, Dad pulled Stan free from the muddy suction pit.

Stan and I playing with our rabbits.

Spike jumped up and down and ran back and forth barking in joy. He seemed to realize that he was the big hero and had really saved Stan's life.

As I grew up, I, too, would join Spike and follow Stanley around. Stanley also had a white rabbit whose soft fur and wiggly pink nose I loved. We would feed him carrots and clover when available. However, one day I remember seeing the rabbit lying very still on the ground. This would be my first brush with death. He did not run or hop. I remember Stan had tears in his eyes as he dug a deep hole under the peach tree. He picked the bunny up and carefully placed him in the hole and covered him with dirt. I suddenly realized we would never play with the little rabbit again. It brought a hollow feeling and copious tears. Stan tried to console me.

To change the dreary mood that day, Stan got permission from Dad to let us go down the road to the Guard House at the outpost, which divided the civilian side from Fort Andrews. On the way, we walked by Sam Perry's house, and his son Leo joined us. Leo had been added to the Perry family at six weeks old. His birth mother was a girlfriend of Connie's from Puerto

Rico, and had separated from her soldier husband. She had been working as a live-in maid on the Post and could not keep Leo. He was never, to my knowledge, legally adopted. But, for all intents and purposes he was the Perry's son.

The three of us were on our way to the pigpen, which was in back of the outpost Guard House, when we noticed the sentries walking their post from one end of the beach across the isthmus to the other beach, meeting each other half-way. The sentry on the Guard House porch yelled hello to us and asked what we were up to. "Just looking at the pigs," we said. We stood by the fence and watched the porkers root and wallow in the smelly mud. Leo reached under the fence to fetch a piece of turnip. He thought that if he climbed up on the fence, he could see better and throw it farther and the pigs would run grunting and honking. Great idea. Except that as he threw the turnip, he lost his balance and fell into the mire. The two big fat pigs made a beeline toward Leo. With their snouts, they rolled him over and over in the mud. He had no chance to get up and run. His screams brought the guards running. They dragged Leo out of the pen, an unrecognizable, smelly, muddy mess.

We were sent high tailing it home, knowing full well aware of the music that we would have to face when we got there. Connie and Leo's sister, Vi, stripped Leo in the back yard, and scrubbed him with buckets of water back to a recognizable state. He was then sent to bed. We soberly watched, delaying the moment of confrontation at our own house. Stanley explained to father what had happened.

Dad said, "Well, for annoying Sgt. Fred Perry's pigs, you must stay inside our fence tomorrow. No kids are allowed inside or outside. Now I will give you some chores to do."

The next day we spent inside the "compound" with chores and no outside distractions. Dad watched us from the front window of the shed.

A few months later, the pigs were slaughtered. I remember seeing them hanging from a high cross tri-pole in the Perry's yard. When I saw them hanging there, I was horrified and ran home bawling my eyes out. Dad punished me because I had been told not to leave the yard on that day, as well. I would have been spared the scene if I had not disobeyed. Stan tried to explain to me that the pigs had been raised for food and they had to be slaughtered to provide food since meat was so very expensive.

Adventures with Dad

Often in the summer on Sunday afternoons Dad would dress in a three-piece suit, starched shirt, gold watch and chain, and straw hat. Mother would dress me up in my favorite dress, one covered with hand made French knots, white shoes and socks and the usual big bow in my hair.

We were then ready for a walk up to the Post to the parade grounds. Sometimes there was a band concert or a dress parade. I loved seeing the soldiers march with a row of flags blowing slightly in the breeze. There was the bugler and the band with its big tuba going ump–pa–pa and the other instruments glistening in the late afternoon sun. Then they would

The parade grounds were our first stop to see the soldiers in formation and flags flying.

Sundays were for dressing up and taking a stroll around "The Rock."

call retreat with the booming of the salute gun, the bugles sounding the call of retreat and the flag being slowly lowered. It was a very inspiring occasion, even for a child my age.

I always insisted that we go behind the headquarters building to the small field where the barrage balloons (short fat observation blimps) were anchored. From our house we could see the two big fat olive-drab sausages floating in the sky, looking out to sea. They were a residual of the late war. To me they were awesome and fascinating, and it was fun to walk under them. We would also stop at the bakery where they were making Monday's bread and goodies. Soldiers love kids, so I always made out like a bandit with cookies, a raised doughnut — the kind my Mother did not make — or, of all things, lady fingers. They were as light and fluffy as angels' wings and oh so good.

Fresh baked loaves cost only two cents!

Bread, hot and crusty, fresh from the oven, was only two cents a loaf. Dad would buy our next day's supply.

Sometimes we would go in the opposite direction through the big stone and concrete arch at the outpost onto the civilian side. The arch resembled a western Army outpost gate. At the time of the building of this arch, there was a small internal war on the Post. There were those who wanted the arch and those who did not want it. The commanding officer won out and the arch was built. As we walked through the arch into the civilian side of the Island, we would sometimes pass Joe Cabrelle's cows wandering on the hill munching here and there. I would always pass them very quickly. I never could quite trust those big brown eyes.

The cows really lived off the fat of the land. All the hills

In the background, the arch defines the border between the civilian and military sides of the Island.

were devoid of vegetation with the exception of lovely soft short wispy grass and a bayberry bush or a wild rose here and there. On a spring day, we would see blue and white violets, yellow-eyed blue grass and pink clover pop up everywhere. Joe Cabrelle, the cows' owner, supplied almost all of us with unadulterated, unpasteurized whole milk, put into cans and bottles that were hastily rinsed in cold well water. I never heard of anyone becoming ill from the milk. Only when the cows got into the bogs and ate the skunk cabbage was the milk intolerable. It took me almost 20 years before I could drink a glass of milk without smelling it first. But then, as a child, I disliked milk on general principles, anyway. When we would return from a walk, it was good to sit and rock a bit on the front porch, often with guests since we always seemed to have company.

It was about 1922, and Father had been retired from the Army for four years. However, in 1918 the War Department had granted him permission to remain and maintain his home on a garrison Army post once his request was discussed by both houses of Congress. Some years later when Sam Perry and Sergeant Fred Perry (no relation to one another) retired, they too were granted the same privileges.

Now retired, and Mother busy with Post activities, her sewing group, the house, we children, and a million other things, Dad would keep his eye on me while Stan was at school. Other children on the Post who were not yet in school were sometimes invited down to play with Leo Perry and me. We would play either in Dad's workshop or in his big iron boat, the *Goldbrick*, which was named after one of the tugs that had towed our house around the Island years before. Dad would put a ladder against the side of the boat and we would climb aboard. It was an open launch type boat about 25 feet long with the motor in mid-ship. It was in need of extensive repairs. Since it was no longer of use to the Army, Dad thought it might be a challenge to repair it, so it was given to him. At the bow, there was a small deck and a window that slid up and down. There was a bell and a horn. How Dad ever survived us kids yelling commands, accented with bells and horn, I'll never know. We all had one whale of a time.

Sometimes if Mom was in Boston, Dad would make lunch and all our young friends would stay. His specialty, among other things, was whipped potatoes, or "spuds" Army style. I don't know what he did to make them so delicious, but the kids always stuffed them away and came back for more, something most of them didn't do at home. Larz Ecquezel, the son of the Post's doctor, apparently raved to his father so much about Sgt. Bies' whipped potatoes that one day the Major Doctor himself knocked at our door. He wanted to know Dad's secret.

There were other times when we would play in Dad's workshop. Dad would give us a block of wood, a hammer and

My dad's workshop next to our house.

nails, and we could pound away; or, he would bore holes in a piece of wood, and give us a screwdriver and a couple of screws to screw into the holes. He was very careful to impress upon us that we must only use wood that he gave us. A few years before, Stanley had very carefully filled the chopping block full of nails. Dad, never suspecting such a thing, went to chop a piece of wood. Sparks flew and so did a small piece of steel from the ax blade. Dad had been very angry but still could not help being amused at the same time. Stan had done such a perfect job of covering the top of the block with nails. Dad cooled off a bit before he explained to Stanley why he must never do such a thing again, and that if he did, he could expect to be punished severely.

We also took turns turning the grinding wheel. It was fascinating to watch the sparks fly, and amazing to us that Dad never got burned by them. We loved scrambling through the wood shavings on the floor to see who could find the longest curl. The winner got to have an extra chance at turning the grinding wheel. We kids would stand and watch almost spellbound when Dad would fire up the forge and put in a piece of metal to heat. When it was white hot, he would remove it with long tongs and put it on an anvil, pound it into the shape he wanted, then plunge it into a bucket of water. Steam would spew forth with a loud hissing sound. When the metal was cold, Dad would retrieve the piece and continue on with whatever he was making. His father, my grandfather had a blacksmith shop back in Poland when Dad was a boy.

Dad had an extremely inventive mind. In October of 1900 he had been granted U.S. Patent #659123 for the first adjustable bicycle or other vehicle handlebars. Unfortunately, he never pursued this project commercially. Some years later when the patent had expired, someone else did use the invention, which became standard adjustable handlebars and doubtless made a fortune for the foresighted entrepreneur.

First Year of Kindergarten

In the summer of 1923 — July 31 to be exact — my youngest brother Eddie was born. I was to go to Grandmother's for several days, and was very excited. Unfortunately, after two days away from home, I was so homesick I became ill and Grandmother had to bring me back home. I was almost hypnotized by the new baby. It was so tiny and seemed to do little but sleep and sometimes cry. I can still remember being very concerned and upset when he cried. Both Stanley and I rocked Eddie in the big rocking chair and pushed him in the wicker carriage; but somehow we couldn't wait for him to get as big as we were.

Mother, with all her chores and activities, plus a new baby, still took time to teach me the alphabet and numbers. Stanley was her assistant. As an aid for learning, Dad had first made Stan letters and numbers out of carefully hand cut and fitted pieces of wood about four inches high. Now it was my turn to use them. Mother and Stan played ABC games with me to help me recognize each letter. There were blocks of different colors for learning the colors. I was ready, as kindergarten was to claim me in the fall.

Stan was an old pro at going to school and so far had survived the many difficulties Army Island kids had in trying to obtain an education. My parents were a bit apprehensive, however, when it became my turn to join the other children. I was the only one going to kindergarten. The other kids were in higher grades. I was rather delicate, very shy and supersensitive. The only time I had been away from home was during the summer when Eddie was born and that had only lasted two days. All day long at school could prove to be very difficult, even though Stanley would watch out for me.

The boat trip across the harbor was routine, but the uncertainty of the boat schedule often made life miserable and challenging for the children. If freight was heavy, or the boat was held at the Army Base for a ranking officer, it could be as late as an hour or more. In early fall and spring, it was not bad being outdoors even if it rained as it was usually warm. In winter it was brutal. The Town of Hull left the school open for us until the custodian had to go home, usually about 3:30. School ended at 2:30. Our boat was supposed to arrive at 5:00. There was no place to go after 3:30 but to the dock. In a biting northeast or northwest wind with snow and sleet, the half-mile between the dock and the school seemed endless. When we got there, there was a huge dark dockhouse. Unfortunately, the Army did not open it until a few minutes before boat time. Anyway, being outdoors was not much different than being inside temperature–wise, since the huge potbelly stove was seldom fired up. One year, the big dockhouse burned and a small one was built. The new one did not make much difference because it was still not usually accessible to the twenty or so children.

My first school picture.

My first few days in kindergarten were a disaster. I felt very grown up, but I was kind of homesick and afraid. I was very quiet and too shy to ask my teacher, Miss Ross, if I could go to the bathroom. I tried to get my courage up, but when I did, it

Mother had her own stationery as the postmaster for Peddock's.

was too late. I made a puddle on the floor. The children were all very quiet. They just stared, no snickering, no laughter, no taunting looks, just silence. I started to cry. I had to sit off in the corner by myself for the rest of the day. Never did I make that mistake again!

By the time I was going to school, Mother became Postmaster. I think I enjoyed it as much as she did. She insisted on being called Postmaster. She said she was no one's mistress. Her day started at 7:30 a.m. Any new mail that had been dropped in the slot after Mother left the post office the night before had to have its stamps canceled, recorded, and put into its proper packet en route to the South Postal Station. Her mail orderlies were the current buglers who had mail duty as a special assignment. They would take the mailbags to the dock for the morning and afternoon boat pick up and drop off.

I would usually leave home early with Mother, especially in the winter, before the boat left for school. She would pro-tect me from the biting wind and snow that blew in from the northeast and the open sea, especially at the top of the hill. Our house was sheltered by the hill from the northeast, but the top of the hill, where we had to cross, was wide open. The wind would literally blow my breath away, and to counteract this, I would breathe through my mouth only to have my breath blown back down my throat and make it feel like a burning fire was taking over my bronchial tubes and lungs. Mother would open her long coat and envelop me. We would both stumble along, often through two or three feet of snow, and head down until we got into the lee of the first set of quarters on the Post.

A one-cent stamp

Down the road were the headquarters and the comfort of the post office. After a brief warming up, Mother's orderlies would walk me to the boat. In the evening when we would get home from school, I usually stayed at the post office. I would do my homework, endure the teasing from the soldiers, and help Mom cancel stamps on the outgoing mail. Mother's pay was based on the number of stamps cancelled plus a nominal monthly fee. There was no set salary. Letters cost two cents to mail in the 1920's. So, even with five or six hundred people on the Post, it was not a big income, especially in the summer when most of the soldiers were on maneuvers.

The position did have other compensations. Mother knew everyone on the Post and knew everything that was going on. She made many friends, and though she never availed herself of the privileges, she did have the freedom and privilege of riding in the officer's cabin on the boat and could ride in the officer's wagon. Being Postmaster had prestige and respect.

After Christmas, the weather was almost more than I could handle with the cold winds, the ice, and snow. Dad would sled me to the dock from home, but it was the walk on the Hull side that was unbearable. These were the days of long winter underwear, the kind that bunched up and wrapped around your ankles. Over these, you pulled on long black stockings and the bumps on your legs at the ankles made you look deformed. High shoes that laced or buttoned to just above the ankles were worn under clumsy black buckled overshoes. The girls wore only dresses with two starched petticoats. Girls did not wear slacks. Even though horse-drawn snowplows had plowed the roads, there was still snow on the roadways up to a half foot deep. The overshoes made a great receptacle for the

Vi and Bill Perry model the type of bulky winter clothes from the 1920s.

snow, and often by the time I got to school I was shivering and soaked to the skin up to my middle. The nurse, Miss Duggan, or my teacher would take me into the teacher's room, remove my long underwear, now mottled by the black dye from the stockings, and put them on the radiator to dry. I was wrapped in a sweater, or whatever was available, and left by the radiator to thaw out and dry.

Unless there was a noon boat, the half-day of waiting after kindergarten was over was so endless and tiring. Even though I was allowed to wait in the school until 3:30 I had little to do. After lunch, I looked at books, played in the sand table and sometimes joined the first grade class. The older kids fared better than I did. But, I would just reassure myself that next year I would also be older.

New Neighbors

Our neighbors were constantly changing, as happens on most Army posts. The house next to Sam Perry was bought by Sergeant Tommy Quinn, after he was bumped from his quarters on the fort by someone who outranked him. Sergeant Quinn had been married to Nellie while he was on duty somewhere in Russia. They now had two children, Tommy and Jimmy. Nellie spoke English fairly well, but had great difficulty understanding American culture and our rather casual approach to life. Perhaps that was why her two American born boys teased her and played tricks on her.

In the mid-twenties, Nellie's mother came from Russia for a visit. She was a topic of conversation on the Post. I do not know much about her arrival, but I do remember her. She was medium tall, substantially built with high cheekbones and a tanned and very lined face. She was stolid, unfeminine, but had soft sad eyes. My first close encounter with her was one day when I climbed on the picket fence surrounding the Quinn's large beautiful and bountiful vegetable garden. Tommy and Jimmy, who were a year or two younger than me, were snickering and peering around the corner of the house. Every once in a while they would fire a small pebble at their grandmother. She would run after them muttering in Russian, but could never catch them.

I sat there fascinated. She was like no one I had ever seen. Her feet were bound in rags and burlap bags. She had a long dark skirt on, and a dark colored baggy blouse tied around her middle with a rope. Her hair was hidden and held quite securely by a white cloth pulled straight across her forehead, folded over at her temples and tied under her chin. The rest of the cloth was draped over the back of her head and then tied around her neck with a piece of cord. I stared at her while the two boys kept peeking around the corner of the house. I wondered what the old lady was going to do when she saw them. She ignored them, and they eventually disappeared.

I finally got up my courage and said, "Hello." She looked up from her digging as though she had just noticed me and said, "Allo" and waved her hand and went back to her work. I stood there and watched her. Tommy and Jimmy called to me, and reluctantly I climbed off the fence and went over to see what they wanted. The boys did not cotton to Grandma. She spoke no English, was a no-nonsense person, and showed no outward affection; so they were almost afraid of her. Consequently, they tried to antagonize her. As time went on, they became more accustomed to her, and though awed by her, they became a bit more relaxed and more or less accepted her. Their grandmother never squealed on them for throwing stones and their mother never caught them. The old lady seemed to make no demands. She would work in the garden from sunup until sundown with time out for meals. She sometimes did a bit of cooking, and won my admiration with some very delicious delicate deep fried puffy pastry that was sprinkled with confectioner's sugar. She never went to any Post functions with Nellie, and communicated only with the immediate neighbors. Sign language and a word here and there at least conveyed friendliness. Eventually, she returned to Russia.

There were other older visitors to the Island who we would encounter as young children. We were first introduced to our

We are posing above the climbing roses with Dad holding Eddie and Stan standing behind me.

new commanding officer, Colonel Leonard, by happenstance via his mother-in-law, who arrived on our steps in the middle of June. The air was heavy with perfume from the roses that now covered our porch. Stanley and I were pulling weeds from a flowerbed and watching our baby brother in his playpen when we heard a small voice say, "Little boy, may I sit on your porch behind all those beautiful roses?"

Rather taken by surprise, since we had not seen anyone, Stanley stood up and faced a very elderly and frail looking lady. He hesitated and quietly said, "Yes, Ma'am" and went to open the gate. He assisted her up the two granite steps to the porch and then fixed a pillow on a rocking chair where she sat down. He sat on the chair beside her. Not to be left out, I quietly sat on the chair that was left. We did not see Mother surveying the scene from the front door. No one spoke for a moment. Then the lady opened the conversation saying to Stanley, "Now little boy, my name is Mrs. Lyons, but I don't bite. What is your name?"

Stanley studied her for a minute and in his quiet way said, "Well Ma'am, my name is Stanley Bies, and I don't sting."

Mrs. Lyons had apparently walked down the road away from Colonel Leonard's quarters in the officers' line. By now we all had telephones, so when Mother discovered her identity, she telephoned the Colonel's wife, Mrs. Leonard, suspecting that perhaps the elderly lady had wandered away. She was right! The Post was in an uproar. The CO's mother–in–law was lost; perhaps she had fallen and was hurt. Mrs. Leonard was very grateful and thanked Mother when she learned that her mother, Mrs. Lyons, was safe and was happily having tea, cookies, and conversation with Stanley. After a rest in the rocking chair, Stanley and Mother walked the 90-year old lady home. From this little incident a friendship grew between Mrs. Lyons, the Leonards, and us.

Catherine Leonard and I, who were near the same age, became good friends and would play together frequently. That's when I got to know Catherine's governess, Mary Louise Beverstock. I suspect I loved Miss Beverstock as much as Catherine did. Miss Beverstock took us on nature walks, acquainting us with weeds, flowers, trees, insects, etc. We went swimming, picnicking, sliding, skating and skiing. She taught us art, music, diction, and manners—not to mention correcting our English. I spent as much time as my folks would allow at the CO's quarters during the year and few months when they were all stationed at Fort Andrews.

Mother so admired this family, that she broke her long-

The Commissioned Officer's quarters where we would often play.

standing rule about sewing for other people, and began to sew for Mrs. Lyons. Mother was the only one, including Mrs. Leonard, who had free access to the elderly lady's room that housed her five beloved cats. In spite of this wonderful rapport, it is to be remembered that there was a great difference in our status: that of a commissioned officer of the highest rank and that of a retired noncommissioned officer.

We were reminded of our status when every now and then, we would play with the children who lived in the quarters on the Post. We would sometimes be invited to the Post to play, and afterwards, Leo Perry and I—seeing we were close-by companions—would have to get permission from our parents to pass through the arch at the outpost and leave Fort Andrews on our own. With a note to the sentries, we were on our way. We liked to walk way over to the West Head past the civilian side of the Island to pick flowers. It was rather a long walk since we always took short detours on the way to follow a bird or look for big toads. There were lots of little toads, but we liked to hunt the big ones.

Along our way, we would stop to say "hello" to Mr. Perry Silva. A handsome white-haired gentleman, Mr. Silva was weather beaten and tanned by years of lobster fishing in the salt air and sun. He spoke so softly and gently that we loved to talk to him. He and his wife were quite poor, but they always had a goody for us. Their tiny cottage had so very many flowers out front and was neatly painted inside and out. The three rooms inside were spotlessly clean. The iron cookstove was polished till it sparkled, and the linens on the table were crisp and white, as was the bedspread on the bed. It was truly like a doll's house.

After our visit, we would continue on our way to the West Head. As we passed the inner swamp, we would stop to see the minnows and strange water creatures in the brackish water. Once in a while a white heron or two would be standing on their long legs in the swamp fishing. Soft wispy grass grew on the Head and was ankle deep. There were no trees, maybe a bush or two, with a few weeds here and there. However, just over the crest on the down slope of the southwest side of the hill, was a carpet of purple with the violets we had come to gather. It was very beautiful and very quiet. The lone house on the Head, called "The Clubhouse," which was reputed to have been the scene of some wild parties, was not often occupied.

Down near the beach as the hill flattened out was a rock maybe two feet high and three and a half to four feet long. One day as we sat quietly watching the water and slowly gathering violets, there was a loud whir as a tremendous bird flew over and lit on the rock. We watched it fold its wings. It was bigger than any bird we had ever seen. Its head was white with a curved beak and a white tail that was slightly spread. It sat quietly, slowly turning its head. Leo said, "Gee, it's not a hawk or a snow owl. It's too big and besides, it's brown. It looks like an eagle." We decided it was an eagle. Suddenly, we became frightened. It was so huge and we had heard stories of eagles carrying children away. We picked our violets up and started to run. The movement frightened the bird, and it took off toward the mainland in the direction of the Blue Hills (in Milton). We took off toward home! We were breathless from running and excitement. On the way home, we met old Joe who had also seen it. He believed it was indeed an eagle. He had seen it once before. When we got home, we were bursting with the news and told everyone who would listen. It was an experience I vividly remember. Many years later after not having seen Leo for 20 years, almost the first thing he asked me was if I remembered the day we saw the eagle.

The Civilian Side

Our other "neighbors" on Peddock's were the early settlers of the Island. These native islanders were moved onto Middle Head once the Army took over the East Head to estab-lish Fort Andrews. These civilians were now separated from the East Head by the Outpost, the arch where sentries stood guarding the demarcation. We would refer to their side as the "civilian" or "summer" side, and sometimes as the "village." Many of these civilians were of Portuguese descent, and made their salaries off the fruits of the sea: lobstering.

These residents had relatively free access to the Fort and its boat service. Several of the village children went to school with us, making the long trek daily across the flats and up the hill to the dock in all kinds of weather, subject to the same dif-ficulties that the Army youngsters faced. We all carried our lunch in tin boxes and often traded sandwiches, but only if theirs were made of delicious homemade Portuguese bread. At Christmas and Easter, some of the village families had open house with all kinds of special goodies. Most of the families were devoted Catholics. I remember always seeing a small altar with a sparkling white altar cloth, vigil candles, a cross, and at Christmas a crèche in their homes. The welcome mat was out to all, though some cottages were especially popular if they had a spot of free good cheer on tap for the grownups.

The village was a close knit group of Portuguese lobster fishermen. In the early 1920's, each dawn from March to November, the men would row their pods (a sort of double-ended boat) out as far as Boston Light in all kinds of weather to hand haul their heavy wooden traps. They made these traps with hand tools during the winter months. The fishermen patiently knitted the heads (where the lobster crawls into the trap) with tarred manila rope, which was about an eighth to a quarter of an inch in diameter. These heads were fitted with a heavy wire hoop about six to eight or more inches in diameter. Two of these heads were then tied into the trap. The trap was weighted with a brick or two and soaked in the sea for a week or more. Wooden blocks were hand carved into buoys, painted in identifying colors and attached to the traps with 100 or

The Civilian Side: Middle Head of Peddock's Island on the east facing shore towards Hull.

My father with a "neighbor" from the civilian side of Peddock's.

more feet of tar treated manila rope. The stacked traps were loaded onto the pods to await being baited with smelly old fish and then dropped into the sea.

Lobsters were quite plentiful during the 1920s in Boston Harbor, and the week's catch was put into a car (a large sea storage box) to await the weekly row all the way to the Boston market. People were very honest, so I never heard of anyone stealing from a car. Before rowing home, bait was purchased and stowed aboard for the coming week of fishing. It was back breaking, time consuming work with relatively small returns, since lobsters were only about twenty-five cents per pound retail. During the summer, lobster was almost a staple in our diet due to the generosity of the Portuguese fishermen. Mother tried to show her gratitude by giving gifts of tea, coffee, sugar, rice, and flour in ten-pound lots which the fishermen and their families in turn appreciated.

There were always funny stories being told about incidents on the civilian side. Old Joe Gill was a fisherman who had a great sense of humor, with many stories. He once told a story about himself when his wife and their three youngsters were ashore on the mainland overnight. His wife had left food for Joe in the icebox such as freshly made kale soup, fresh bread, linguica, and hash. Joe would tell the story that he came in starved from fishing. He went to the icebox, dragged out some of the food and gulped it down. He was so tired that he did not even heat it. It tasted great cold, especially the hash. There was nothing better than his wife's Portuguese bread. He ate a good bit of that as well as the kale soup, which was another favorite of his. He ate everything.

When his wife returned the next day, she had dinner ready for Joe when he got home from fishing. She asked him if she had left enough for him to eat and if it was good. He replied that everything was fine, especially the hash.

She asked, "What hash? The can I left for you is still on the shelf."

"The hash in the bowl," said Joe.

"Oh, Joe!" she said. "That wasn't hash, it was dog food. What did you feed him?"

There were many other stories that originated from the civilian side. As one might imagine on a small island, storytelling ran rampant about the many islanders who tended to be amusing, almost bordering on the eccentric. Characters, perhaps. Names like John Irwin, "The Widow," and the Rallahan family were among the characters we'd hear about.

John Irwin, an attractive looking gentleman who seemed rather quiet, owned and operated the Island Inn, also known as the "Headache House Hotel" which was the center for adult entertainment in the early 1900s. Irwin's establishment was reported to have had excellent food, fine wine and liquors, and very beautiful women—all available to the patrons who arrived daily by boat, which landed almost in front of the hotel. The clientele was not that of the Ritz by any means, so there were brawls and murderous fights, which often necessitated summoning the mainland police.

After one such escapade, it was said that Irwin was allowing a gambling establishment to exist. He was arrested and banished from the Island, asked never to return. The hotel was closed and eventually fell into disrepair and ruin. The memories of wild times, beautiful women, good food and drink were entombed in the molding, crumbling rubble of the old hotel, leaving only the aura of romance. In later years, we would sometimes see Mr. Irwin, a friendly white-haired gentleman, on the mainland of Hull, where he lived after his banishment from Peddock's. He would sit on the front porch of his house on Main Street, always greeting us with a smile and a wave.

"The Widow" (whose real name was Mrs. Curran, or Currier—I never really knew her actual name) was another character we would always hear tales about. As a little girl, I helped my mother deliver mail to her. She was a heavyset lady, well groomed, a beautiful face with pale complexion, jet black hair and impeccably dressed though always in black. It was said she buried two husbands, each of whom left her reasonably well off. It was also said that a soon to be retired soldier, one Sergeant Paul Bork, became an ardent admirer. He proceeded to move in with her, which was in those days a shocking event, generating much gossip. This arrangement lasted a number of years until Sgt. Bork passed away. After his death, The Widow became more and more eccentric.

Gradually she became increasingly careless about her appearance and her house. She rarely, if ever, bathed; she smoked cigarettes chain fashion; and her clothes were anything but clean. Eventually she closed all but one room of her house and lived only in the kitchen. Her four cats were her constant companions and even shared her dinner plate. Only a few islanders were allowed in her kitchen, where a whiskey bottle was always nearby. She never seemed to lose her faculties in spite of her frequent visits to the bottle. She was caustic but witty and never wasted words. It was said she paid her bills

Sam Perry waits for his next customer beside my grandmother's 1925 Nash.

promptly, and in some ways, she was very methodical. She had even made her funeral arrangements, even down to the kind of dress she wished to be buried in. These arrangements, I was told later, were completely paid for. It was not until several years before she died that I really became acquainted with her during one of our Friday shopping trips.

The Army out of Fort Banks (Winthrop, MA) provided "L" boats for a once a week shopping trip on Fridays, principally for the various Army caretakers. The civilians were allowed to use the boats and we all took advantage of this privilege. The Friday shopping trip seemed to have a holiday atmosphere. In good weather Sam Perry, with my grandmother's old 1925 Nash, ran a taxi service of sorts on Peddock's Island. Sam would drive around to the civilian end and pick up as many people as he could. This was gratis, of course. The Widow was always a passenger since her weight encumbered her walking abilities.

Sam's "taxi" service ceased during the winter. So, on one

winter Friday, when there was a heavy coating of ice over the deep snow and walking was extremely difficult, The Widow lumbered along fairly well until she reached the hill headed up to the dock. Unfortunately, as she was walking up the slope, she slipped and fell landing heavily on one knee. By the time they got to the mainland, her knee was twice its original size and she could barely walk. With Sam's First Sergeant style of insistence she reluctantly, and under protest, went to the doctor. She balked at taking off any of her clothes, but the nurse took matters into her own hands and The Widow undressed at least to her underwear.

After the examination, the nurse showed The Widow back to the waiting room. With an amused smile she told Sam that there were no broken bones, but that Mrs. Curran was badly bruised and swollen and would require rest. She confided that she understood the woman's reluctance to undress because, besides being very unclean personally, she had made her underwear out of flour sacks; not so unusual in itself, but who would want someone to see the big red letters across the front: *Use No Hooks!*

Another name that seemed to generate colorful stories on the Island, was the Rallahan family. The Rallahan house was a small house at the base of the hill between the Serrilla cottage and the McGhee's house. The Rallahans had lived there a number of years with their two pretty daughters, Dottie and Virginia. There was a bit of a commotion when it was alleged that John DeAvilla, who was married to Mary Lewis (the daughter of an island lobsterman) was paying more than casual attention to Dottie. Rumors were that Mr. Rallahan, who had a tube in his throat, supposedly the result of cancer, had threatened to shoot Johnny if he did not leave his daughter alone. Johnny was never shot in spite of the threats, so I assume he ceased his attentions. Virginia, the other daughter, was a pretty girl with a beautiful body. She went on to become

Ginger Waidron, a stripper and the toast of Boston burlesque. She played the Old Howard and the Crawford House which were Boston's famous burlesque theaters at the time.

Overall, there were always the stories to keep us going. Whether there was validity to them or not, I'll never know, but without the stories, island life might not have been as colorful. It was these kinds of stories that we grew up on, and brought flavor to an island that was better known for its military maneuverings, than its civilian natives.

Preparations and
Military Maneuverings

As expected, Army artillery was ever present on Peddock's Island, so most of the Army children were taught how to carefully handle small arms and ammunition at a young age. Father was a fine marksman, and eventually we were taught how to fire a .22 rifle and a light pistol. Dad would set up a target against the big hill. Mother was perhaps Dad's worst student. Some years before when he was teaching her to shoot, Mother's fear of the weapon caused her to aim too high and the bullet shot up through her bedroom window and shattered the huge mirror on her mahogany dresser. That was the end of Mother's target practice. Otherwise, practice went on every now and then. By now, Stanley had graduated to the point where he was allowed to fire Dad's old Colt from his Fort Apache days. This was an occasion, and the Colt was handled with great care and respect. It was Father's most valued possession. He told many stories of the gun's importance in the prairie lifestyle of the Army, civilians, and the Indians in the West during the turn of the century. It was as famous as the Sharps rifle, which the Apaches favored.

I also remember loving to sit and watch the military maneuverings, which happened in the hollow 50 yards from our house. It was almost like watching sulkies getting ready for a race as the mules and the caissons would get into position for

Stanley (standing in the middle with a rifle) learned at an early age how to shoot a rifle.

practice action. A rat-a-tat volley of machine gunfire would start and could last from ten minutes to half an hour. A guard would run a red flag up the flagpole near the outpost guard house warning all not to walk into the line of fire. After a day's firing, the kids would scavenge the hollow for shell casings. Occasionally we would find live ammunition that was returned to the Army. The casings would later be sold for junk.

Other maneuverings would go on, but the real excitement came when the big mortars that had been returned and replaced after World War I were fired. Fort Andrews would need to be prepared and secured for the coming practice action. The huge guns were cleaned and greased. Magazines were opened and projectiles were rolled out. The plotting tower at the top of the second hill was in full action. Telephone lines to the gun pits were all go. Far out in the harbor beyond Boston Light, the area was secured from shipping. An Army boat, often our favorite, the *Jessup*, towed a tricone-shaped target on a long

The soldiers prepare for the military maneuvers set up on the hill behind our house.

cable. On the Post, all the quarters were secured by removing pictures, dishes, and breakables from the walls and shelves, by packing them into boxes or putting them on the floor. Otherwise, the repercussions might damage them. The Post population not actually on duty—wives, children, etc.—found a place to sit on the hill high up and away behind the gun pits, near the plotting tower. We could see every bit of action going on below as well as hear every command from the plotting tower that was repeated on a megaphone down in the pits.

We patiently waited for what seemed like hours while all the procedures were coordinated. Finally, the long awaited command came to raise the muzzle of the gun to be fired and get ready to aim. This produced a lot of action in the pits. First ramming the projectile and an eight-pound bag of powder into the breech. Next, the command to "Fire." Wow, what an experience! Flames were everywhere; at the breech end was fire; at the muzzle end was fire; the grass on the hill of the pit slope caught fire. Then with a tremendous "Barroom!" the whole Island seemed to shake and shudder as the projectile went flying. Dead silence in the crowd! We couldn't see the missile until it splashed in the water, throwing a geyser 100 feet high, short of

Soldiers on the hillside positioned to fire during a maneuver.

the target. Sighs of disappointment from everyone. Action again in the tower and in the pits; orders to change the position of the gun so many points in a designated direction. Again the command, "Ready....Fire." "Barroom!" A second shot was off, this time dead on target. Cheers went up from the spectators. Three more shots as the target was moved further out in the Harbor. Two made their mark. The third hit the water just a smidgen short. The afternoon was a success. As cheers went up again, the crew in the gunpit took off their fatigue hats and threw them in the air.

Preparations were already under way for tomorrow, and perhaps an even more successful day of practice. All firing was not without its mishaps. Once, faulty calculations sent a projectile through the wheelhouse of an Army towboat. Fortunately, only one man, the first mate, was injured. Splintered wood and glass were embedded in his right hand and paralyzed it. This injury prevented him from becoming a boat captain. He received recognition and compensation. But instead of retiring on disability as he could have, he elected to remain on the boats as first mate. Such was the stuff of which these men were made.

Troubling Boat Trips to School

With each fall came the problem of the children from the Post going to school. There was agitation among the officers and enlisted personnel for a mini school on the Post for at least the first four grades. Fort Strong on Long Island was part of Suffolk County and it had an elementary school with Miss Alice McNally as teacher. She was provided by the City of Boston. Constant appeals to the Town of Hull, Plymouth County, for a teacher for Fort Andrews fell on deaf ears. Many incidents precipitated the clamor for an on-island school. There were often hours of waiting in the freezing cold for a boat due at five p.m. but arriving Hull at 7:30, or later, long after dark. At times, the inability of the boat to make it down the Harbor in a fierce storm, left the children stranded, and having to be put up at Fort Revere in Hull, sometimes for a couple of days. There was no time for play; no time for school activities. These all played a part in the wishes for a school on the Island.

Though the children rarely, if ever, got into trouble, accidents did occur. I remember the time little Davy Crockett (a descendant of the original Davy Crockett) was playing "Hide and Go Seek" on the boat. We kids had been told not to cross the gratings over the boiler pits where the funnels came through the deck. In the excitement of the game and running to avoid being caught, Davy darted from port to starboard across the gratings. One of the gratings was not firmly in place and down went Davy, twenty feet below, onto the steel bulkhead of the boiler room. He lay motionless as the astounded fireman, who was just about to empty the boilers of the fiery coals on the exact spot where Davy lay, stared in disbelief. He scrambled to pick Davy up. The kids were yelling, "Davy fell down the boiler room. Davy fell down."

The boat guard came running. There was silence for a moment. Everyone was afraid Davy was dead! Not that fiery little redhead! As they brought him up the steel ladder to the deck to check for injuries, he kicked and squirmed and cried, "I wanna get down. I wanna get down. Let me down." He looked at himself, black from head to toe with coal soot and he started to bawl.

Thinking he was hurt, the boat guard said, "Davy where do you hurt?"

Crying even louder, Davy squawked, "I don't hurt anywhere, but when I get home my backside is gonna hurt. My pants are dirty!"

Children from Peddock's wait for the boat to take them to school in Hull. I'm the blonde, one child in from the right, with the tie.

Children in Harbor Forts Severely Handicapped in Their Attempts to Obtain Adequate Schooling

Left to right, top: Boston's novel public school at Fort Strong, Long island, Boston harbor. These army children pupils and Miss Alice McNally, who conducts the school; the Fort Andrew school at Peddock's island; an army post activity for the 12 little ones at Forts Warren and Andrew. Harvey S. Van Brocklin, teacher (standing). Below: The little gray schoolhouse at Long island.

Younger Ones, Especially Have Their Own Difficulties

By CHARLES A. PARKER

"It's different if you happen to live in Boston within a stone's throw or a few blocks of a public school! Bill and John and Mary can race into the breakfast room, grab a brace of eggs, whip on their hats and be off to classes within 10 minutes of the opening bell.

UP BEFORE DAWN

A group of youngsters whose fathers direct the destinies of Uncle Sam's Boston harbor fortification activities or are employed on the harbor islands must hop out of bed as early as 6 A. M., before daylight dawns in winter, in order to make their Boston school classes.

Others, younger children, also, have to be fed, bundled up by anxious mothers in harbor island homes an intrusted to the tender mercies of steamer captains while the children make a twice-daily trip to and from another island for their schooling.

Still another squad of youngsters depart every school day morning from their homes in the army barracks at Ft. Andrew on Peddock's Island for classes in the Hull intermediate school.

Mothers and fathers and their children of the harbor have their troubles as to schooling.

The romantic tale of the farm boy who arose at dawn to tramp miles to the little red schoolhouse for his training in "the three R's" sometimes pales into insignificance beside the struggles of the harbor island boy and girl in getting his or her requisite schooling.

SCHOOL NEEDS ACUTE

School needs at Peddock's Island, across Hull gut from Pemberton point, became so acute that the different army officers and enlisted men with children have now organized a school there, in a wing of the army hospital building. Under the guidance of a young first-class private, Harvey S. Van Brocklin, former newspaper man and Culver Military Academy graduate, 12 little ones, nine from the Andrew post and three from Ft. Warren, are getting their training in the first four grades.

It is a miniature school; a post activity, but somewhat an adjunct to the Boston public school maintained at Ft. Strong, where 16 harbor island children, mostly from Strong, attend the "little gray school building" there under the tutelage of Miss Alice McNally, who must go and come via the institutions or the army steamer daily to her task. Miss McNally is a regular Boston school teacher.

Dick and Austin Ryan, sons of Supt. John J. Ryan of the Long island (Boston) institutions; Charles Leonard, son of Lt.-Col. Charles F. Leonard, executive officer at Fort Andrew, and George Maize, son of Sergt. Maize, at Strong, share the steamer trip to and from

Boston with another group of boys and girls now attending the South Boston high from different harbor forts. The first four attend the Boston Latin school.

NO TIME FOR PLAY

Parents of both groups lament that the children have practically no time to cultivate their school friends or take part in school activities. The young people, however, seldom express pessimism because of this necessary school traveling.

Harbor island parents' worries crystallize over school difficulties, however, at Fort Andrew, from which post eight boys and girls daily make a trip across Hull gut in the army base steamer to attend school at Hull.

The group has outgrown both the Peddocks and the Fort Strong school. Its members are not yet old enough for high school, however.

From the Hull government wharf the eight walk about a mile to the Hull school.

Recent enforcement of new government economies now restricts the government harbor boat service to two round trips daily from the army base to the islands and back.

BOAT OFTEN LATE

While the boat is due at the Hull wharf for the school children there as

Forced to Wait Hours for Boats Under U. S. Economy

early at 4:30 P. M., it is often 6 and sometimes as late as 7:30 before this group of little ones are picked up for their trip back home.

The situation is causing worry and alarm among the parents of this group, and is rousing a strong sentiment on the islands in favor of appeals for a public school at Andrews that would accommodate the higher intermediate grade pupils.

Such an appeal has been made in vain to the Hull school authorities. The district is in Plymouth, not in Suffolk county.

Hull school officials, however, have authorized the keeping open of the school building there for the convenience of the waiting harbor children. But because of the frequent delays in the arrival of the boat the boys and young girls are forced to wait on the lonely wharf too often in the cold and very frequently close to or after dark.

WAIT FOR HOURS

The Hull school is out at 2:30 P. M. All the boys and girls leave via the steamer around 3 in the morning and seldom reach home again before 5. It is too often much later than that.

Col. William K. Naylor, commanding the 13th infantry at the harbor forts, himself stationed at Fort Andrew, feels that the establishment of a school of the higher intermediate school grades at Fort Andrew would solve the vexing problem even in years when pupils from the other posts than Andrew required these high classes, "for," the colonel declares, "there could be a more careful supervision of these boys and girls while they were waiting, if they were at the post here."

January 29, 1927 article about our inadequate schooling situation.

One of the many boats that broke through the icecakes around Peddock's Island so passengers could get to Hull.

Then there was the time in mid-February, 1925, when I was about eight years old. The harbor was full of ice cakes when Leo, now about six, fell overboard. He was talking with the engineer, Pat Delaney, who all the kids liked, when someone yelled, "Hey Perry, don't you get off at Andrews? You better get going 'cause we're leaving the dock."

Leo started to run from mid-ship to the bow and the gangway, not looking to see that the gangway was on the dock, not on the boat. He ran right overboard and fell between the ship and the dock. The Jessup's steam turbines were immediately cut to prevent the huge propeller from turning and the suction from pulling Leo under and perhaps cutting him to ribbons. Leo was floundering in the icy water. Everyone was yelling and life rings went flying through the air into the water when a middle-aged soldier jumped into the water and grabbed Leo.

The soldier secured his arm through one of the life rings, still holding onto Leo. The soldiers on the dock pulled both of them out of the water and up onto the dock.

Having only seen Leo fall overboard, I went running up the road from the dock screaming, "Leo drownded, Leo drownded."

I got home breathless, crying my eyes out. Barely five minutes later, two soldiers and Leo came running over the hill. The soldiers had Leo between them holding his hands and running him so fast his feet barely touched the ground. Sam and Connie popped Leo into a tub of lukewarm water and gave him hot whiskey tea (Sam always had a store of contraband on hand). Leo never even got a cold out of his winter swim. The soldier who saved him got some kind of a medal, and Leo gave him a jackknife. I guess this was a kind of preparation for Leo's later exploits in World War II when two of the Navy ships he served on were torpedoed and left him swimming first in the North Atlantic and then again in the Pacific. He got the Navy Medal of Honor for going back to his burning ship and rescuing several of his shipmates. He went on to become a Navy frogman and performed some dangerous and daring undersea work during the Korean War.

We were constantly at the mercy of the weather. One January morning, when I was in the third grade, the *Jessup* picked us up at around eight o'clock.

A northeast wind was whipping up. It was about 25 degrees and very cloudy. Ice and snow were on the ground from a previous storm and there was light slushy ice in the bay. As the day drew on, the wind picked up and it started to snow. The Point Allerton Coast Guard facing Boston Light, then on the seaside of Allerton, had hoisted gale-warning flags.

A group of us left school about three o'clock and made our way in blinding snow to the dock, hoping that perhaps our boat would come early because of the storm. We huddled together on the lee side of the dock house where the eves pro-

The crew of the Jessup, *one of our favorite army boats.*

truded a bit, offering a little shelter as we tried to keep warm. About 4:30, the wharfinger, who was in charge of the dock, arrived in a snow covered wagon drawn by two mules whose blankets were covered with icy snow. Clouds of steam from their nostrils were being quickly dissipated by the wind. As the dock house was opened, we all crowded to get in. The cold had gotten to all of us. It was cold inside, but what a relief to be out of the vicious wind and icy snow. The thirty more minutes before our boat was due passed rather quickly.

It was getting very dark and the wind was whistling a mournful tune. Around six p.m., the dock phone rang with the news that the *Jessup* was having difficulty but had made it to Fort Strong, the first stop out of the Army Base in South Boston. They hoped to proceed directly to Hull to pick us up, not stopping at any other forts on the way. It had been ten hours since we left home in the morning, and we were tired and hungry. One of the soldiers who was also waiting for the boat had some crackers which he passed to us. We grabbed them like vultures. We tried to play games and sing, but everyone was apprehensive and rather on edge. The news arrived that the *Jessup* could not make it and was stuck at Fort Strong.

We were told, however, to stay at the dock because the captain of the *Executive*, the Army Engineers Boat, had volunteered and promised that, "No damn Northeast gale would prevent him from getting those kids home or he'd sink trying."

Around nine p.m., the wharfinger, who had built a fire in the stove to warm us, saw the dim lights of a boat bouncing crazily but heading for the Hull dock. The tide was dead low. Ice covered the pilings and the gangway drop was frozen tight at the high tide level. The *Executive* was a tug type ship with a cut off cabin and a tall boom, often used to lay cable. It was wide and deep in the water, and even in a fierce storm had a certain amount of stability. The *Executive* approached the dock almost head on. It was very difficult to see the dock lights in the blinding snow. A deckhand flung the hand line, which the wharfinger scrambled for and barely caught. Two other soldiers helped to haul the icy hawser to the dock and secure it to a bollard. A second line was secured to the stern. The *Executive*'s ice festooned deck was a least fifteen feet below the useless gangway drop. The ship was tossing and heaving, and the gangway could not be used. We would have to negotiate a ladder to reach the deck. In the pitch black of the night, one by one, the kids were slowly climbing down the icy runged ladder.

My turn came. The wind and sleet were slicing my face. I was shaking so, my boot slipped. Terrified, I hung suspended on an icy rung. I could hear the angry water churning below. I hung on for dear life, frozen with cold and fear. Suddenly I became weightless and thought I had let go and was on my way to falling into the dark, angry sea below me. Someone had grabbed me and I found myself in the warmth of the wheelhouse. Tears were falling in abundance, my only defense from fear. The *Executive*'s Captain Joe Bannanas had a way with children and soon he had dried my tears and more or less calmed my fears. Finally, we took off on a short but very rough trip across the bay. There was great difficulty in landing, but eventually we made it. The Fort Andrews' children were home and they all slept in their own beds that night.

Hull had but one school in the twenties named The Village School, which was on Spring Street across from the Fire Station. It went from kindergarten to the eighth grade (high schoolers took a bus to Hingham High School). The Village School was a small school but a very good school with very devoted teachers. Clarence V. Nickerson, a gentle dignified man, was the principal; and the two Misses Bowdens, Davies, Southworth, Ross and Studley were teachers I fondly remember. Who could forget Mrs. McGlaughlin, the gym teacher who was always on our backs to stand up straight?

The Town of Hull took very good care of the health needs of the school children in the late 1920's. Miss Duggan, the school nurse whom I held in awe, was tall and very pretty. When she weighed and measured us, she looked very important in her crisp blue uniform with its white starched collar and cuffs. Dr. Sturgis, of whom I was terrified, was the school doctor. He explored our throats with the horrible stick called a tongue depressor, took our temperatures and checked our eyes and ears. The school dentist, Dr. Derby, had an office on the second floor with all his "torture tools." Just to have a tooth and mouth examination, for me, was another name for panic. I avoided even going by his office if I could.

My third grade report card, carefully preserved by my mother, provides a stark contrast to report cards of today. I read it with considerable interest and found that not only was there an academic learning process, but also a character building learning process. Character building was placed under the title of Citizenship, a way in which the teachers helped us to make one a credit to ourselves, our family, community, country, and all of humanity. Citizenship was broken down into many areas in which we were graded: manners, courtesy to teachers and associates, consideration for the rights of others, cleanliness,

The Hull Gala Days took place right on the grounds of our school.

civility of speech, respect for law, order, and authority, responding to directions, respect for yours and other people's property, patriotism, willingness to render public service, care for books, and, finally, posture in sitting, walking, and standing. These were some of the things we were taught within citizenship. To us it was very important as it reinforced our parents' teachings and their desire to build good character and good citizenship. This list was added to double grading in academics (one for class work and one for tests) and made our report cards very definitive. There was a very close feeling between the faculty and the students, a rapport that I still remember. One example of the concern for the students was that the teachers always stayed at least an extra hour and kept below average students after school to upgrade their marks.

Class size was at least 30 to 35 students, yet no one had difficulty learning. Discipline was adhered to, if necessary, but self-respect and respect for the teacher and anyone in authority practically eliminated punishment. The teachers knew how to teach and made learning interesting and desirable.

The climax to all our school activities at the end of the year was the big pageant on Hull Gala Day: a spectacle that townspeople, Army people, and everyone enjoyed. It was held in the playground in front of the school. All the school children participated, with costumes, group dancing, and formation marching. The Color Guard carried the flags, while songs and music were provided by the 13th Infantry Band, who donated their services. It all ended at about 4:40 p.m. in time for all the Fort Andrews' residents to make the boat for home. These wonderful pleasantries helped soften the many hardships the Island Fort children endured.

As time went on, boat service to and from Hull to the islands became limited, so few island people would attend the Hull Gala Day events. Of course, everyone throughout the Boston Harbor Islands would enjoy and marvel at the railroad lights display at night when the Town of Hull was outlined with red railroad signal lights from Pemberton Point to Nantasket along the Hull Gut side as well. The lights were spaced about ten feet apart, and burned for about a half an hour. It was like a fairyland. I never could quite figure out how it was accomplished, but I well remember the beautiful spectacle. I was rather young, and the engineering aspects never entered my mind. But in my adult life, I have thought about it and wondered how all the signal torches were lit at one time. Seeing so many lights outlining the land with its hills and flat areas certainly left an everlasting impression.

When we heard that the government was going to abandon Fort Revere in Hull, we knew that soon there would be no boat service to Hull. Parents worried even more. Boston was the only alternative. In 1927, when Colonel "Wild Bill"

CO "Wild Bill" Naylor got us the Island School we needed.

Naylor, then Commanding Officer at Fort Andrews, decided to crack the whip, an island school was established. For a time, it was under the supervision of Harry S. Van Brockline who was a first-class private, a former newspaperman and a Culver Military Academy graduate. There were four grades, and classes were held in a wing of the hospital. Colonel Naylor was not satisfied with this arrangement, but it was a beginning. His nickname of "Wild Bill" was bestowed on him for a reason, and when he got wild enough, all hell broke loose! Things began to happen. The Town of Hull finally sent us a teacher, one Ann Tarausi, a tiny, cute, petite slip of a girl with an infectious personality, a sense of humor and a hearty laugh, but with the authority of a general. All of us loved her immediately.

When it was first announced that Miss Tarausi would arrive from Hull and would require a family to board with, there were no takers. The fear was that she would be a sour old maid who would be difficult to satisfy and hard to handle. Mother was at her job in the post office located in the headquarters when the Colonel passed by on the way to his office. He hesitated, then turned back and asked Mother if she would take the new school teacher as a boarder for a few weeks until other arrangements could be made. Mother agreed, but only for a few weeks. Her day was full of activity and she felt she could not do justice to a boarder. Ann stayed with us for only about three days. When the Post families saw her, everyone wanted her to stay with them. She ended up staying with Commissary Sergeant Ross Chesney, his wife, Dixie, and their three pretty girls, the oldest of whom was but a couple of years younger than the teacher.

Ann set up school, again, in the hospital wing. All grades were together in one big room. We, who had taken the boat trip for even a few short years, missed the excitement of the trip, but going to an on-island school was novel and less hectic. I was now in the fourth grade. Ann was a good teacher, and handled the room full of children like a first sergeant.

A little boy named Karl Kupfer, about eight, sat next to me in school and became my admirer, much to the annoyance of my parents. He would be at our door at seven a.m. daily to walk me to school. My father tried to discourage his attention, but since his father was a captain, Dad didn't protest too loudly. The association broke up when Karl gave me whooping cough!

I attended the Island school for just about five months, from September until January, when my parents decided I was on too friendly a basis with the teacher. I spent much of my time with the Chesney girls (Eleanor Chesney was one of my best friends) and our teacher, Ann. Young Army girls were quite comfortable with older girls. After all, there were very few of either. My mother would tell me that I was "too familiar with the teacher to learn." There was no longer a boat to Hull, so I was sent to the O. H. Perry School at City Point in South Boston, and entered the fifth grade. There I met fellow students from Spectacle Island. They were children of the keepers of the two lighthouses on the island and other workers from the rendering plant. We all called them "the kids from Boney

We took a boat to South Boston Army base, and walked from there to the Perry School at City Point.

Wards" since Spectacle Island's original name was Wards Island. The island also had an incinerator at the plant where people from the islands and Boston would send their garbage and dead animals on a barge to be disposed of. Thus, the nickname, "Boney Wards."

It was a long boat trip to the Army Base in South Boston. However, there were older high school kids, including my big brother Stan, Mary and "Boy" (Fred, Jr.) Perry, Eleanor and Dorothy Chesney, and kids from Forts Warren (George's Island), Strong (Long Island), and Standish (Lovell's Island) who went to Southie High. So, I didn't mind the trip. We still had most of the old problems of late boats, cold, snow, and wild storms as well as a long walk across the wide open Army Base to the street car line at the L Street bridge. In winter, it was miserably cold and the wind was like cutting knives as it swept across the open concrete area; not a time to dawdle. In spring and fall, it was a pleasant and interesting walk.

Summertime on the Rock

There was always excitement of some sort on the Post! For weeks in the early summer of 1925 the Post was in an uproar. Everything was being G.I.'d for a major inspection. Barracks were scrubbed and polished; big guns painted and shined; grass manicured; and soldiers were coached in protocol. The President of the United States was going to make a visit to our Post, considered to be the most beautiful in Boston Harbor. President Calvin Coolidge had been Governor of Massachusetts from 1919–1921 and was undoubtedly familiar with Fort Andrews. He chose our fort to review the harbor defenses of Boston. Submarines had proven themselves in the late war and the Port of Boston was vulnerable. Later, the forts in the harbor must be ever watchful and ready to act against any attack from the sea, yes and from the air—the new challenge.

Anti-aircraft guns were installed in the Harbor along with strong searchlight units. These lights were hidden underground in magazines and were run out on railroad tracks when they were to be utilized. The entire installation on Andrews eventually deteriorated and gradually, when the hill eroded, tumbled into the sea.

The day of the visit arrived, July 10. Excitement was indescribable as the President disembarked and hesitated on the dock. A presidential salute of 21 guns was fired by the little salute gun next to the flagpole. All the official amenities of his

Men dressed in the uniform of the day preparing the mortar.

office were tendered to him: honor guard, inspection parade, flags, and music. Then all the official bigwigs toured the Post.

A demonstration of preparing the gun for action was to take place at Battery Whitman, the most modern emplacement on the Island. Soldiers were sweating in full dress uniforms: which, in those days, were made of heavy olive drab wool with high collars, tight breeches, and wrap leggings. Every man was in his place to perform his appointed duty. Everything went according to plan. Each performer was doing an admirable job. Suddenly Sergeant Hipp, formerly our next door neighbor, who was demonstrating how to elevate the muzzle, tripped over his legging that had decided to become unwrapped and caught on a projection of the mortar. The Sergeant turned scarlet with embarrassment, strove to apologize, but became flustered and incoherent. President Coolidge—being a kind, cool, and calm New Englander—quickly put the man at ease, and the demonstration proceeded on to its conclusion. Sergeant Hipp was an impossible act to follow and his fellow soldiers never let him forget it!

Also, during that summer, most of the companies left on maneuvers. Lighters pulled away from the dock laden with footlockers, small arms, caissons, horses, mules and other equipment. They were bound for Fort Devens in Ayer, Massachusetts, and for Ethan Allen in Vermont, along with the companies for Forts Warren, Standish and Strong. The boat schedule was completely disrupted, as it would be again in the fall when they returned. For us, this would mean hours of waiting to get home from school. Of course, it was great when it worked in reverse and the boats and lighters arrived too late in the day for us to get to school.

There was a small crew left behind to keep the Post going. A quartermaster, commissary and bakery crew, stable men for the animals left behind, as well as some administration personnel. Shortly after the departure of the Army companies, the National Guard would arrive with all their equipment. Barges and boats going and coming provided lots of activity. The National Guard took over the fort for two weeks and lived in tents.

After the National Guard's stay at Fort Andrews was over, came picnic time at Peddock's Island. S. S. Pierce, the famous Boston grocery store, had a huge picnic for its employees at Fort Andrews. It was almost like a carnival. There were all kinds of contests, games, prizes, spun sugar, taffy apples, ice cream cones, hot dogs, buntings and flags, music, dancing, and singing. What fun and excitement! But, best of all, it was free for kids! People and freight were brought over by the summer chartered Nantasket boats—we called the *Nans*. It was wonderful to have the *Betty Alden* and the *Mayflower* dock at our dock. They were civilian boats! The ladies would arrive on the Island in summer voiles and organdies and floppy straw hats. The men were dressed in linen suits or white flannels with Panama hats or stiff straw lids—very far from the informality of today. Everyone seemed to be having a genuine good time.

One of the Nans.

There were tons of food and beverages. It was Prohibition, so there was no "legitimate" spirits evident, and the Post was well guarded, so few, if any people got to the civilian side to the bootleggers. When the S.S. Pierce party was over about eight p.m. or so, the *Nans* would arrive and carry the people and debris away. Picnic time would be over as well, and the Post was back to normal until the next year.

From April until November, the *Nans* were a source of life to the whole area. The elegantly decorated, beautifully maintained, picturesque steam side-wheelers were owned and operated by the Nantasket Steamboat Company. They ran an hourly schedule from Nantasket and Pemberton to Rowes Wharf in Boston. There was also a narrow gauge train which made boat connections and ran from Nantasket to Pemberton making stops along the way at Stoney Beach, Kenberma, and Allerton. The tracks and stops ran along the Hull oceanfront and afforded a beautiful view of the open sea and Boston Light.

Pemberton was a lively place until the late 1920's. The huge Pemberton Hotel was famous for its hospitality and its food, especially its shore dinners. It was popular with the elegant people of the day. The Pemberton Inn was a small intimated place that sat behind the hotel, and survived until the 1930's.

The many sections of Hull: Pemberton, Allerton, Kenberma and Nantasket.
Peddock's sat about a half-mile west off of Pemberton Point.

The Hotel boasted a steam-heated, salt-water swimming pool. There was also excellent food and dancing. After Prohibition, they could serve liquor. It was a very "in" place to go to dine and dance. Toward the end of its reign, it was a real swinging spot. Interestingly enough, Hull High School now sits on this piece of land that harbored the high life of a by-gone era.

The Town of Hull was at that time a wealthy summer resort with many important politicians and rich business people, who took up residence in both the summer and winter. Most commuted to Boston daily on the Nantasket boats. There was no more elegant, peaceful, and pleasant way to travel, and all for only twenty-five cents from Pemberton and fifty cents from

The Pemberton Hotel once sat where Hull High School now stands overlooking Peddock's. The Inn sat to the left of the hotel.

Nantasket. Over the years, the prices increased, of course, but were generally affordable for all. In winter, there was a bus connection that eventually arrived at the elevated trolley— then called the "El"—to Boston. There were many small business people in Hull who often used the bus.

The Islanders made very good use of the boats and started to depend on them. Several summer residents, who lived on Peddock's Middle Head, commuted from The Rock to Boston jobs daily. Each workday boat was sure to see at least a half dozen regulars on their way to make the 8:15 a.m. boat to Rowes Wharf. They would return on the 5:30 p.m. boat. Sometimes the weather would foul the schedule, but a pretty good commuting record was maintained.

The Army side of the Island had a couple of regular commuters, too: the Post's painter, Anthony Reis who lived on the mainland and from whom we bought our cabin cruiser the *Matilda*; and our neighbor, Sgt. Clark, who was attached to the Army Base in Boston. In summer, they both preferred the *Nans'* regular schedule compared to the Army boats' unpredictable timetable. Soldiers and their families kept Mr. Huer-

Dad with friends on his boat the Matilda.

son, the first civilian ferryman for the Army side of the Island, very busy since he lived on the base. I remember he was also the Post's plumber.

Huerson 's ferryboat, the *Divine*, was in less than good condition. The garboards, which are wooden planks on either side of the keel, were dry rotted, and some of the ribs were split, so she leaked badly. Mother and our neighbor, Sgt. Clark came home from Pemberton one evening very late in the fall. Huerson, a man who liked his "tea," was "three sheets to the wind," and the actual wind was blowing up from the northeast. The trip was rough. Water came in bucketfuls over the bow and through the floorboards. All three of them were sloshing in water over their ankles. The boat was low in the water and laboring. It was touch and go as to whether they would make it across Hull Gut. Sgt. Clark turned white as a sheet and was speechless. Mother, who was no swimmer, clutched one of those cumbersome, old-fashioned cork life preservers, thinking any moment they would be in the drink treading water. The *Divine* must have guided them. The old Mianus engine kept chugging as they bounced and inched their way to the dock.

The ferry dock at Fort Andrews.

They were soaked to the skin and shaking. Dad had been pacing the pier nervously watching from the Fort Andrews side, feeling totally helpless except for numerous prayers.

Commuting season was almost over and the boat would be beached for the winter. Huerson's career as a ferryman came to an abrupt end as he had orders to leave Andrews for another fort. He sold the boat, and after a couple of interim short-term owners, our neighbor, Fred Perry, bought it.

The Huerson boat, in spite of several repair attempts by the interim owners, was still leaking very badly. Fred was aware of Dad's competence and ability and wanted the boat repaired properly to be safe and seaworthy. Dad went to work replacing the garboards and putting in several new ribs. He built a steam box with complicated molds to bend the oak pieces into proper shape. Next he sliced the wood into the proper thickness and curved it with an adze. The garboards then had to be painstakingly fitted into their proper position next to the keel of the boat. Then the ribs had to be bent and riveted to the hull. We kids watched him in fascination as steam hissed and chips of wood flew.

The following spring when the *Nans* would arrive, Fred Perry's boat, newly named the *Jack*, was ready to go back into service. Fred did a good business for several years. When his Army service interfered, his wife ran the ferry very efficiently, which was very unusual in the 1930's. In the 1938 hurricane, the *Jack* broke its mooring, dodged all the islands and shoals, and landed practically unscathed somewhere in Gloucester Harbor. It was returned to the Island and eventually retired. Later the Jack was burned and its ashes scattered on the sea. This was a very fitting tribute for an old and faithful servant.

Boat Services

There were other boats that also caught our attention, such as the rumrunner boats, since some of them I would see docked at the Army Base in South Boston, near the school I attended. The rumrunner boats were constantly being caught and confiscated by the government and brought in by the Coast Guard. Some of these boats were battered and riddled with bullet holes from their chase with the revenue boats. It was exciting to imagine and speculate all the action of the capture, and all of us would conjure up all kinds of tales. The coves along the north and south shore provided secret places for the rumrunners to hide or unload their contraband. Once in a while when they were in a close chase with the revenue boats, they would dump their cargo overboard. Sometimes the hooch would wash up on the various island shores, and I heard that some of the Island natives would find a bottle or two of prime rum or scotch. My parents never found any, but there were always tales of other island folk who had access to spirits during this era of Prohibition.

During the 1920's, the civilian end of the Island had quite a flourishing bootlegging business going. Soldiers, it seemed, would drink anything from Listerine to rotgut. I'm not suggesting that the Peddock's Islanders sold inferior booze. I think most of it was pure, even though flavored and watered down as far as it could be and still be alcoholic. It was apparently good enough for some of the men to risk court martial and to engage in any ploy to get by the guards at the outpost. There was an old serenade that the GIs sang that went like this:

> If you ever come down to Fort Andrews and
>   want to get in with the bunch,
> You better come down quite early and don't
>   forget your lunch.
> The boys down here are starving. It's a terrible
>   remark to make
> That Hogan wouldn't run the marathon for a
>   half a pound of steak.
> We have no pie, no ham to fry, the place is on
>   the bum,
> The boys are going to the village trying to get
>   some rum.
> The rum they sell in the village sure is extra fine,
> It's good for cuts and bruises and better than
>   iodine.
> If you ever get up in the morning and your head
>   is full of pain,
> Just take a drink of the village rum and you will
>   never wake up again.

In order to find this ill-fated hooch, the soldiers would hide on the beach and wait until the guards met each other half way on their walking post, then sneak by the barbed wire fence, which extended to the tide line. In summer they would take the civilian ferry from Pemberton, or sometimes a friend on guard would allow them to pass and pretend not to see them. Come hell or high water, where there was a will there was always a way to get what you wanted. Enough of the fellows found their way over to the other side to make it profitable for the purveyors.

The Portuguese fishing folk on the civilian side had their "merchants" as well. All summer Rosie Alberts, who lived in Crab Alley (the section of Middle Head overlooking West Head), cooked her lobsters and crabs outdoors on an old iron cook stove that was parked right in front of her house. She sold the shellfish and the booze to wash them down. Rosie spoke little English, but this was no barrier to business. She married Mr. Alberts when he went to Portugal to find a bride. When he returned with Rosie and her little boy, he was asked about the boy, and it is said that Alberts retorted, "Well, when you buy the cow, you have to take the calf."

The Goularts also did a flourishing business, and their pretty daughter did not hurt business either—even though it was a case of "look but no touch." There were others who got into the act also. The hooch was often consumed on the spot, or one could buy an unmarked bottle. Bottles were kept in a false wall or floor and often in the "Kazinger"—popularly known as an outhouse. Sometimes they were hidden in the ground or a wood pile—any place that would secret them from the "Revenuers." Whenever they showed up, there was never any evidence to be found.

The king of the bootleggers, Eddie St. John, lived in the first house on the civilian side with Joe Stafford, who was a bootlegger's assistant. There was a sweet, lovely teenage daughter, Gracie, and mother, Mrs. Stafford who made life miserable for all of them.

Sunny Smith lived next door to the Staffords in a small house and distilled the booze when the coast was clear. One Sunday evening in the early fall, our family was having early dinner with a couple of soldier guests prior to going to the movies at the Post Exchange (PX). From our dining room window we saw a column of smoke rising from one of the summer cottages straight across the flats. Our meal was left on the table and we all took off across the flats. Sunny Smith's still had

The Portuguese fishing folk on the civilian side lived in these cottages on Middle Head overlooking West Head.

blown up and his cottage was going up in smoke! The flames were like fireworks on the Fourth of July with shades of green, turquoise, red, yellow, and orange shooting skyward.

The trick was to save the other cottages. There was little water because the wells were very low after a dry summer. A detachment of soldiers from the Post arrived by mule team with brooms, buckets, and burlap bags. Civilians and soldiers, men and women, manned a bucket line and kept as steady a stream of water on the fire as they could. Others beat the burning grass with wet burlap bags and brooms. The wells were drained dry, but they finally succeeded in extinguishing the blaze after only two cottages burned. This mishap did not, however, dampen the spirits—both emotional or liquid. The people made and sold spirits as usual as soon as the smoke cleared!

* * *

Boats were part of our lives. Without them and their crews we could not have functioned. Our two favorite Army ships were the *Jessup* and the *Bachelder*, named, I think, after generals.

Soldiers and deckhands on the Bachelder.

They were by no means cruise ships, but they afforded us a warm and comfortable space to sit in the winter and plenty of deck space in the warm weather. We also had limited space to run and play, though it was not always appreciated by the deckhands and guards who did their best to keep us safe and reasonably quiet.

The greatest respect was shown to the boat captains. The *Jessup* had a kind but no nonsense Captain Bill Coughlin whom the kids greatly respected and admired. He would allow us to go into the wheelhouse—sacred territory—and examine all of the fascinating equipment, as well as turning the wheel. This was a big thrill to kids. The second *Jessup* captain, Hollywood, was not too receptive to children and his abruptness turned them off.

Happy-go-lucky, gray haired and almost rolypoly Captain Hodgkins, who never seemed to be bothered by kids, was in command of the *Bachelder*. We did not ride his boat as regularly as we did the slightly larger *Jessup*. In spite of school transportation difficulties, we had compensations on the boats. When we were hungry, there was always food going to the Army mess on all the forts, and the deckhands took advantage of it. They would open a 100-pound burlap bag of potatoes, and the fireman would take them to the bowels of the ship and roast the critters in the fiery coals of the boat's boilers. One definite advantage coal had over oil. The potatoes came out practically incinerated. The black charcoal was about one-quarter inch thick on the outside, but they were pure white and luscious on the inside—even without butter.

One very windy evening, there were huge boxes of oyster crackers on deck as part of the cargo. A tremendous 50-pound box went crashing down and split open on the bulkhead. Blown by the high winds, the oyster crackers mimicked a snowstorm pelting and peppering the ship. We children were in heaven with crackers up to our knees. We filled our lunch boxes, our pockets and our hats. We ate and ate. Then, we couldn't get enough water to quench our thirst!

There were minor accidents now and then, but there was one real tragedy that I remember. One winter night, the wind was blowing gale force. Snow and sleet was falling, making the deck a frozen sheet of ice as slick as a skating rink. It was pitch black. A tall, quiet, young soldier deckhand left the central cabin to cross the frozen deck to go to the crew quarters below. He never came back, and was not seen again until his body was found on the beach at Fort Strong about a week later. It was so wild out that night that the captain on the bridge could not see what was happening on the deck just below. He never saw the soldier go overboard, and if he had cried out, the captain could not hear him.

There were lots of fun times, too, especially when the spring brought the sun and warm days. We would sit on the upper stern deck watching the sea and the birds, play games, read, or just talk. Sometimes we would sing, and sometimes drive the guard on the boat nuts by running and playing hide and seek. There were always people from other forts on their way to or returning from Boston, so there was a great deal of sociability on the long trip. Most of the time there was a lot of freight, which would take time to unload at the different stops, so the hour trip usually took two hours.

All of the civilian work force traveled on the boats, including some of the Army Engineers, one of whom was Franklin "Red" Pierce. Red lived in Winthrop, and I guess everyone knew him for his outgoing friendliness and gift of gab. Red always had a yarn or two to spin, and always had an amused audience when he was spinning. Edward Rowe Snow, the late harbor historian, lived on the same street very near Red. Snow begged Red to take him down the Harbor on the Army boat that was not readily available to non-Army or Army related personnel. Pierce's yarns so intrigued young Snow, who was a school teacher at that time, that he became curiously interested in these Army islands and their stories. The first time I heard Snow's story of "The Lady in Black" (the Civil War "ghost" of a woman who was hung for the attempt of freeing her Confederate husband from the Fort Warren prison on George's Island) was from Red. This, we assumed, was one of Red's yarns. He often worked at Fort Warren on George's Island in the batteries, casemates and dark dungeons. Red's historic facts were embellished and fantasized. Anything for a story, so Red's gifts of imagination plus fact were engineered into yarns for anyone who cared to listen. Mr. Snow became a familiar face on the islands for the next fifty years. Usually, islanders would politely avoid him and his numerous questions.

Social Events and
Seasonal Activities

Social events throughout the Harbor Islands were always scheduled to keep island life fun. Saturday night was dance night. The different forts took turns hosting the dances. Ladies from social organizations in Boston as well as girlfriends of soldiers, etc. were invited. Mother took me to the dances at quite a young age, but generally I was only allowed to attend those held at Fort Andrews.

The dances were held in the gym that was decorated with flags and banners. It was a spring, fall and winter activity, that was very well attended, and a family affair. Ladies arrived with their children, even babies. The balcony over the gym provided a rather secluded place for them to sit and watch the dancers below while their babies slept in carriages nearby. When the mothers wanted to dance they would pop down the stairs while one of the other mothers would watch the babies. They would dance up a storm, then pop back to allow someone else the same privilege. It was a great arrangement.

Come intermission, they would serve coffee, Army doughnuts, and once in a while cake. Sometimes we were lucky enough to be invited to the bachelor sergeants quarters just up the hill from the Post Exchange on the Officer's line. Provost Sergeant Toby Lyons would have a tasty buffet whipped up. He was a tall, well-built, middle-age, handsome bachelor as well as an amateur chef. He prepared food that was as beautiful as it was delicious. Often it was lobster in some form, a jellied salad, homemade bread or rolls and desserts such as you would not believe. My friend Eleanor Chesney and I were always first up the hill.

Eleanor and I felt very grown up in our fancy dresses. I loved pretty clothes, and Mother made me many. I particularly remember a dusty orange, pure silk taffeta dress covered with ruffles. I felt like a queen, especially when some young soldier I knew would ask me to dance. All the grown-up girls — Gertrude, Vi, Mary, Edna, and others — always had dance partners. They were very popular with the young soldiers. Army sons rarely seemed to be interested in the dances. Mother could not bribe my brother Stanley to attend, and Eddie was too young to be interested, and none of the other boys ever seemed to go. The girls from ages nine to ninety were always there. Few of the ladies from the Harbor Islands ever missed the dances.

Jo Costello, a very athletic, dark-haired young woman, whose father was the caretaker of Rainsford Island, took great risks to get to the Fort Andrews' dances. Of course, there was a tall, good looking young soldier, Charlie East, who may have been the magnet. Rainsford was across the harbor from us. Jo would leave the security of their beautiful big rambling white mansion on the hill, jump into her canoe and paddle the long distance across the Harbor to Sam Perry's house where Charlie would meet her. Weather or time of year did not seem to deter her. She almost always made the dances. There were times when everyone thought she was loony to attempt the trip when the weather would be at its worst. Jo was an excellent swimmer, and in summer she would swim the distance for fun.

Other social events were planned throughout the year. Once a year, the Harbor Women's Club sponsored a big costume ball. Mother usually planned it and was the hostess. She was treasurer of the club, which supported the Women's Ward at Fort Banks Hospital in Winthrop. At this time, the Army did very little for Army wives and children. They did, however, provide a hospital room, doctors, and nurses. The Harbor Women's Club members provided most of the medication and all of the maternity needs. These special dances, such as the costume ball, raised a great deal of money for these needs. All of the soldiers contributed, and bought the thirty-five cent tickets for dances willingly, since the regular Army dances were free.

The costume ball was a gala affair. The gym was decorated in a very lavish manner with buntings, flags, and huge bunches of colored balloons that were suspended from the ceiling. The balloons were released to float down on the crowd after the Grand March. There were door prizes, favors, first, second and third prizes for best male and female costumes. There were special raffles, including a gorgeous triple tier cake made and decorated by the Cooks and Bakers School on Fort Strong.

Many of the costumes were unusual, and some were very beautiful. Soldiers and families who had lived in foreign lands often had native costumes from those areas. At one ball, the Hawaiian wife of Sergeant Lewis wore a real grass skirt and danced a hula. Among the costumes, there were beautiful hand embroidered outfits from the Philippines, gorgeous robes from China and Japan, colorful Mexican skirts and pants, and even a fur parka from Alaska. As you can imagine, the judges always had difficult decisions to make. Sandwiches, coffee, cake, and ice cream were served at intermission. At midnight the orchestra played "Home Sweet Home" to signal that the dance was over. The Army boat—either the *Jessup* or the *Bachelder*—was at the dock ready to take the dance crowd back to Boston or their respective forts.

Dances were not the only winter diversion. There was basketball with an inter–post championship at stake. We had our

Eddie, as a toddler, standing next to one of Dad's boat engines.

favorite players, one being Stanley Chappel from L-Company. He was a tall, very handsome young man from New York. Often he was the guard of the boat, and though he made us toe the mark during our school trips, all the youngsters liked him. He was Vi Perry's (Leo's sister) boyfriend. At that time, she was going to Boston Teachers College. Vi and Stanley planned to marry after she got her teaching degree (and they did).

There was also a bowling alley on the Post, and there were movies two or three times a week. At first, they were silent pictures but had piano accompaniment. Gertrude Perry, Fred Perry's daughter, who was quite musical, was often the accompanist. She married an Andrews soldier named Jack Hall who was in the 13th Infantry band. The first-born of their three children was named Don. He spent a good part of his young life next door to us with his grandparents, Fred and Nana Perry. My brother Eddie and Don were good friends and both liked boats. They spent a lot of time tinkering with boat engines. Don stuck with boats, and eventually became an admiral in the Navy. He was with the *Nautilus* when it made its trip under the ice cap.

In summer we would go swimming, though for me the wa-

I loved to fish!

ter was always cold. I would stay in until I was blue, then sit in the sun until I got warm, and then do it all over again. In those days, we had reasonably clean water in Boston Harbor. When the tide was low, we would pick periwinkles off of the rocks and hunt in the tidal pools for crabs. Our catch would go into big clean tin cans that were easy to find on the beach. A can was filled with seawater and then popped on a small fire built on the rocks. When all was cooked, we would sit on the beach, pick the periwinkles out of their tiny shells with a common pin, crack the crabs with a stone, and enjoy the gifts of the sea.

At least once a week on their way home from lobstering, Mr. Perry Silva or Mr. Rose would drop off a bushel of lobsters for Mother which she and I were addicted to. Sometimes, we would cook them on the beach and eat them right then and there. The savory smell of the boiling crustaceans would tantalize the taste buds, and waiting for them to cook seemed like forever. At least once a year we would have a big clambake. Father did not like lobsters, but loved clams. We would dig them on the beach opposite the Guard House. They were white, tender, succulent mollusks that we would sometimes make up into a delicious chowder. As steamers, they were supreme. On Saturday nights, there were weenie roasts on the beach as well as singing fests. After all the delicious, slightly burned hot dogs and marshmallows were eaten, grown-ups and kids alike would just sit by the beach fire entranced by the flames.

Fourth of July was always a special event for us. The young people on the civilian side would gather wood for a couple of weeks for the night before the Fourth of July bonfires. The summer residents on the civilian side would have a bonfire, and the Portuguese fishing folk would have the other bonfire. Each would strive to be bigger and better than the other. The Army did not cotton to bonfires! To add to the excitement, the horizon in all directions would be ablaze with fireworks, each more beautiful than the last. In this atmosphere, the youngsters would sing, play ukuleles, tell stories, and just sit and take in the sights. By midnight, the fires would burn down and the fireworks would be at an end.

On the night of the Fourth of July, the Tea Room, an island store that served candy and ice cream, would stay open beyond the usual nine o'clock closing time. It was a charming little store with bright flowered drapes and painted round tables for serving ice cream and soda. The candy counter was filled with dishes of penny candy and five-cent candy bars. On top of the counter was a jar of ice cream cones. It was on the civilian side and was operated by Ada Carland, her sister Lillian Grand, and their mother, Mrs. Davis whose husband was a sergeant from the Post's hospital. On July 4, almost everyone would drop in for sundaes, ice cream sodas, soda pop, and candy. Ice cream was a special treat on the Island, since 100-pound chunks of ice had to be carted over by boat to keep the ice cream chests cool. Even if electricity had been available on the other side of the Island, electric freezer chests were not yet

Stan (on right) loved to box in the summer. Here he is with Leo Perry.

in common usage. We all had an icebox that had to be fed blocks of ice. One of my daily chores in summer was emptying the pan of run off water from under the icebox.

In summer, diversions turned to the outdoors. There were band concerts, dress parades, and baseball games. A prize boxing ring was set up in back of the headquarters building where the old observation blimps that I used to love to see were anchored. Prizefights were a weekly inter-Post event. We youngsters had our favorites there, too. We always rooted for Gonzales, a Mexican soldier who invariably won when he was in the ring.

Baseball was, of course, a favorite, and like other sports, was inter-Post. Fred Perry, Sr. was one of the best players in the harbor of both baseball and basketball. Sometimes, even the Boston Braves would play on Peddock's—a great event to be enjoyed by all.

Besides enjoying most of the Island activities and entertainment, which was generally family oriented, the young people had their own responsibilities. On weekdays during the winter there was time for little else but school. After dinner on school days as well as weekends, Stan and I were expected to clear the table and do the dishes. Then there was the inevitable homework. If you were fast with that, or just did not do it, you might be able to listen to "The Shadow" on the radio before it was time for bed. Not doing homework, however, did not pay off! You always caught hell from the teacher and were given extra homework. The usual punishment was to stay an hour after school. That could not apply to us in Boston since we had to make sure we did not miss our boat. However, the teacher would send a note home to our parents advising them of our homework neglect. Then we caught hell all over again. Dad would add extra chores and revoke privileges for a spell on top of that. Not doing your homework had no advantages.

Weekends were different. We always had chores to do, of course, but they were done by noon on Saturday, and the rest of the day was ours. The hill in back of our house was practically devoid of growth except for the orchard area. So this provided a great place for winter sports. Stanley and a couple of his friends had skis. I watched them fly up four or five feet off the ski jump they had made. It looked like fun! Dad made me a pair of skis out of curved barrel staves, and after a good waxing, I made it down the small hill pretty well. My confidence grew, and against my brother's advice I tried the jump. I, too, went flying! Up and away! However, I landed head first in a snowy manure pile. The boys roared with laughter as they came to help me out of my smelly predicament. I went home for a bath feeling like a complete failure. So ended my skiing career.

We also had a toboggan that Dad had made out of huge thin wooden cheese tubs. He straightened the thin curled wood by pouring boiling hot water on it, then applying heavy weights. Next, he let the wood dry; and to strengthen it, he put on side strips and cross pieces of oak. A rope was attached to the front that had been allowed to stay slightly curved. The toboggan was then waxed, and away we went down the hill — three young people at a time. It was fast and exciting, so much

Stan, Dad, Eddie, and me playing in the snow.

so that one of the grownups asked if he could try it. He started down the hill great guns, could not steer the toboggan, and smashed into an apple tree in the only part of the big hill that had any obstacles, the orchard. However, the toboggan was repaired and used for many years.

Dishpanning was another favorite winter sport. The barracks had the biggest dishpans you ever saw. They were made of some kind of metal. We would get a few of these pans, and when snow conditions were just right, one could sit in the pan and go churning lickety-split down the hill. It was great fun, like flying in semicircles! It could be disastrous, too, if you lost your balance and went sailing headlong into a snow bank with the heavy dishpan crashing on top of you.

The coasting was great. Everyone—big, little, and in-between—had a sled. The pattern was to start at the Range tower at the top of the hill where, in summer, we would watch the mortars being fired. Then we would go down the hill over the stairs that had been purposely left snow covered; continue on down the road by the Post Exchange, the barracks, the headquarters, and end almost at the dock. It was a great long coast, to say nothing of the long walk back. After three or four trips down the hill, you were worn out.

We had skating of a sort, but the area was very small. The flat part of the hollow usually had ice. Sometimes the Army would flood it, but the run-off and drainage was too fast to make much of a rink. However, we skated on whatever ice there was, and when we were tired and numbed by the cold, we would go to someone's house for steaming hot cocoa and saltines.

A Fort Andrews' Christmas

Each year when November rolled around, the ladies on the Post would start planning for Christmas. A collection was taken among the soldiers for presents for the children. Each child would write a letter to Santa. Since Mother was the Postmaster, it was easy to intercept the mail for the jolly old man. When requests were tabulated, a committee was picked to do the buying of the presents. There were committees to buy candy and fruit to fill the stockings; others would wrap the presents.

The entertainment committee would round up the boys and girls and rehearse them in recitations, skits and songs, and sometimes little dances. I remember the excitement when we were herded "backstage" on Christmas Eve. Backstage was a makeshift curtain across the back of the gym. The piano and a huge Christmas tree, which had been decorated by the soldiers, were in front of the curtain. The youngsters came from behind the tree to perform; that is, all except me. I took refuge behind the tree and spoke my piece. No one saw me, and they barely heard me.

One year my friend Eleanor Chesney and I were chosen to do a little ballet dance called "The Snowflakes." We rehearsed every weekend for hours under the instruction of a lieutenant's wife who had studied ballet. Our costumes were made out of target cloth, which was coarse, off white, heavy muslin that

At Christmas, the mess hall was decorated in all its glory.

they used to make targets. A wire hoop made the costume stick out just above our knees. It was trimmed with white, fluffy cotton donated by the hospital sergeant, and silver tinsel. The tinsel itched and the coarse muslin was like sandpaper on our skin. Our dance shoes were old sneakers painted with silver paint from the plumber shop. Mine shrank! At curtain time, I could not get my sneakers on! The introduction to "The Glow Worm" was played three times, and only one dancer appeared. I was sitting on the floor backstage fighting with my shoes. Finally, I was literally pushed onstage barefoot. I tried hard to rival "Pavlova," hoping my footgear would not be missed. The floor was cold, and the fallen pine needles stuck into my toes and hurt. I kept looking down at my feet, almost forgetting the music and wishing I could make myself invisible. Finally, the music ended and the dance was over. I disappeared behind the Christmas tree, which was my escape. Eleanor took the bow alone. Little did I realize then how dancing would figure into my life in later years. When I recovered from my embarrassment, I took my place with the rest of the children, parents, and soldiers to greet Santa Claus and receive our presents. There were presents for all, including the soldiers. Many of the presents were contributed by The Red Cross. The kids received a stocking with a toy, candy and fruit that was contributed by Army personnel.

After a group sing of Christmas carols, it was time to go home. Excitement danced through our heads as we trudged homeward in the cold. In the quiet, the snow crackled and crunched loudly under out boots. On the hill, the pines near the warehouse stood like sentinels, and the moon's beams fell on the glistening snow. The twinkling stars seemed so close. You could almost pluck them from the sky. All added to the magical feeling of Christmas.

The next day, Christmas, everyone was invited to the barracks for dinner. The mess hall would be decorated, and there would be a big Christmas tree for all to admire. There would be turkey and all the fixings, goodies of all kinds including candy, nuts, fruit, cakes and pies. Excitement always made me lose my appetite, but I would carry many goodies home. My Christmas would go on for a couple of days.

Lucky Lindy and Other Pilots

Today airplanes fly overhead unnoticed, but in the late 1920's they were a curiosity. Many young men and women seemed to be taking to the skies, including a young American pilot named Charles A. Lindbergh who created a world sensation by flying solo in thirty-three hours on May 20 and 21, 1927 from New York to Le Borget Airport in Paris. He made appearances all over the United States. East Boston Airport, now Logan International, was overflowing with excitement because he was going to make an appearance there. It was sponsored by the Army, which greatly influenced the airport at that time. General Brown, Commander of the First Corps Area, and also a pilot, was presenting Lindbergh with highest honors. There were many well-known people and important Army officials on the welcoming committee including Colonel Leonard, Commanding Officer of Fort Andrews, and his wife. Even Mother got involved in the flying enthusiasm. The Leonards invited my mother and some other Army people to assist with the very special preparations. Mother was delighted. She was thrilled to be presented to and shake hands with Colonel Lindbergh, his mother, and the official party.

Unfortunately not everyone was as successful as Lucky Lindy as I witnessed firsthand. Looking back, perhaps my reluctance to fly reverts to my childhood when I witnessed at least two fatal plane crashes. On account of Lindbergh and

*Lucky Lindy and General Brown after Lindbergh's
famous flight across the Atlantic.*

*Charles Lindbergh's mother, who my
mother was thrilled to meet.*

other young aviators of the time, aviation was becoming more
and more of an interest in people's lives. Islands and waters
seemed to be a magnet, and flying over houses always attracted
attention. One morning we were watching a small open cockpit plane fly overhead, apparently carefree. As it flew over
Hangman's Island, which is a tiny mud rock pile on an island
out in Quincy Bay, the plane plummeted down into the mud
and rock. We could see the tail half of the plane sticking up
straight in the air. The rest of it was buried in the mud. It was a
terrifying sight for my brother Stanley and me who were just
old enough to comprehend the tragedy. Both fliers were killed,
burned alive.

Several months later, a plane flying over Peddock's toward
the spit on the southeast side of the Island, seemed to be having
engine trouble. The motor would sputter, slow down, cough,
start up, sputter, then finally it conked out. With a sliding,

My grandmother in front of the grounded schooner, Nancy, *at Nantasket Beach in 1927.*

crunching, metallic crash, the plane went down into the thick mussel bed. One flyer was buried alive and died. The other survived but was very badly injured. Nearby fishing boats, boatmen, and finally the Coast Guard came to the rescue.

Our family was at Pemberton that day meeting a Nantasket boat to pick up my grandmother. We witnessed the horrible mishap, even to seeing the young surviving flyer being taken to a hospital. Another time, with less tragic results, we

Plane over Fort Independence (Castle Island) just off of South Boston.

were all in the yard one summer afternoon when a plane with a dying engine was loosing altitude. It slowly glided into our cove and landed on the shore. The two aviators checked the depth of the water and jumped in. They were only waist deep. Slowly they guided the pontoon plane to a safe position in the shallow water.

Full of curiosity, we all ran to the cove to see if they were OK and if they needed help. We soon realized that they were worrying about being low on fuel and apparently had fuel line problems. All they needed was a little help to clear the gas line. When the difficulty was solved and conversation was flowing, Mother arrived with lemonade and cookies. We kids were invited to climb on the pontoons and get a look at the cockpit seats and the flying area. What a thrill! After more conversation and many thanks, the two flyers took off skimming over the water in the direction of Boston. We never saw them again.

I remember a much more pleasant association with planes some years later. This incident also took place at Pemberton. An innovative flyer with his plane took passengers for a flight around the bay, for a nominal fee, of course. We decided to have him ferry us to our house at Andrews.

On takeoff from Pemberton Beach, we skimmed out over the water on Hull Bay. It took a couple of minutes to fly over the East Head of the Island, Fort Andrews, and out over Quincy Bay. A sharp turn east and we landed on the water in front of our house. We then taxied into the beach and we were home! I don't think I will ever again experience the great thrill I had flying in that open cockpit plane. A glass shield deflected the wind but allowed the air to rush by and blow ones' hair wildly. Skimming over the waves with drops of water splashing gently on the cheeks was sheer ecstasy. This is how it must feel to be a bird.

Caretaking Status

In the late 1920s, many military forts succumbed to a "care-taking status," which meant that the forts would no longer be active. Forts Standish and Revere had already fallen under this ruling. So it was only in time that the rumors we had heard in 1927 finally came true in August of 1928: Fort Warren was placed on a caretaking basis, and Fort Andrews was next in line.

In September of 1928, orders came from headquarters, and the service companies at Fort Andrews would be interspersed throughout New England. Some were to be shifted to Fort Adams in Newport, Rhode Island, where our Commanding Officer "Wild Bill" Naylor, would be in command. Some of the companies would go to Fort Devens in Ayer, Massachusetts and a few soldiers would go to Fort Strong (Long Island), the only garrisoned Army post left in Boston Harbor. It was a complete upheaval that saddened everyone who had lived at our beautiful fort for even a short period of time.

The Naylor family wanted Connie Perry who had been their cook since their arrival at Fort Andrews, to go to Fort Adams with them. If she went, her son Leo would go with her. Her husband Sam agreed that it was the only viable arrangement. Sam would stay at Fort Andrews and keep the home fires burning. Their daughter, Vi was just finishing Boston Teacher's College, and son Bill had started a job in Boston.

Fort Andrews, on Peddocks Island in Boston Harbor, one of Boston's historic old fortresses, has been ordered placed in the caretaking status, the second of such fortresses to give way to modern methods of defense within a month, as old Fort Warren, on Georges Island in the harbor, was placed in a similar status Aug 30.

According to a notice sent out from the First Corps Area headquarters, the permanent station of headquarters company and service company of the 13th United States Infantry Regiment has been ordered shifted to Fort Adams, Newport, R I, and Fort Andrews goes into discard as an active unit in the country's defense forts on the Atlantic Coast. Col William K. Naylor is in command of the transferred regiment.

This makes the fourth Boston fortification to be placed in the caretaking status. Forts Revere and Standish had been placed on a similar basis before Fort Warren succumbed to new methods.

This means that only two of the old fortifications remain active, Fort Banks in Winthrop and Fort Strong on Long Island.

A little less than two years ago Fort Andrews came into public prominence as the result of a fire in one of the barracks, in which were stored quantities of ammunition. The fire wrecked the interior of the three-story barracks of Company K, 13th Infantry, United States Army.

The island on which the fort is located is about half a mile wide and three-quarters of a mile long. It is somewhat nearer the shore than Fort Warren, which has preceded it into discard.

The buildings now comprising the fortification include four brick barracks, a quartermaster's stores building, a post exchange headquarters, 15 sets of officers' quarters, 15 sets for noncommissioned officers, a hospital, a bakery, a firehouse, a guardhouse and a dock.

The Boston Globe, *September 24, 1928*

Sam, now retired, invited his brother Will to come live with him on the Island. It would be too lonesome to be alone after having had a house full of family. Will would retire from his business, tie up loose ends, gather his possessions, and drive to Hull. He would bring his touring car over on a barge with him.

Sergeant and Nellie Quinn with their two sons, Tommy and Jimmy, were to go to Fort Ethan Allen in Vermont or to Fort Devens in Ayer. My parents and my five year old brother Eddie would stay on the Island, but Stanley and I would live with the Chesneys at Fort Strong for the school year. We would be able to get home on weekends because the Army boat, the *Anderson*, would be making weekend trips from the Army Base in South Boston. The *Anderson* also made the daily trips to and from Fort Strong so we would take that boat to get to school. Fred and Nana Perry were expected to go to Fort Devens or Fort Banks.

Vacating the Post would take some time, but by the early spring of 1929, Mother closed the Post Office. It took just about eight months for the Army to move out lock, stock, and barrel. Meanwhile, my parents realized that year round island living would be impossible. Stan and I and soon Eddie had to go to school. Fort Strong was going to close within the year and the boat service would be reduced. Things were so uncertain at this point, that Grandma and my uncles seldom came to visit unless the *Nans* were running.

My folks were forced to take what money

Here I am standing on the steps of the Post Office, where Mother worked.

they had scrimped to save and buy a house off of the Island. We were in the big Depression and times could not be worse. Money and jobs were scarce. The only bright light on the horizon was for prospective house buyers. In the real estate market, there were foreclosures after foreclosures. Houses were a glut on the market and prices were low. Mother and Dad shopped for several months, and finally found a house in Brookline, a suburb west of Boston, that pleased them and was priced right. The determining factor was the taxes. Brookline had the lowest taxes in suburban Boston. Also, the schools were very good. Within the year, we reluctantly moved some of our belongings from Fort Andrews to the new house in Brookline. The Island was still home base. My parents found a lovely old couple to rent a portion of our Brookline house. The couple could help with the mortgage, and mind the house when we were on Peddock's. However, Stan and I would continue to be the Chesneys' star boarders—until Fort Strong closed and the Chesneys were transferred—with brief trips to Brookline.

Our Brookline house.

We all wondered what the first caretaker for Fort Andrews would be like. We did not have long to wait. Almost immediately, a senior caretaker, one Sergeant John Maykovich along with his wife Mamie and their small daughter Mary Ellen, arrived fresh from service in the Philippine Islands. They were not strangers to the Harbor having been stationed for eight months at Fort Warren (George's Island) from August 1926. After that duty, they returned to the Philippines where Mary Ellen was born. They came to Fort Andrews late in 1929 and moved into the Major Doctor's quarters next to the Commanding Officer's house, and soon made the acquaintance of the few Post residents left.

We liked them immediately, and my parents were happy to discover that John was Polish with the same cultural background as ours. His tiny, young, and pretty wife, Mamie, had been born and brought up in East Boston of Irish parentage. The Maykovich family remained at Fort Andrews for several

Fort Andrews' pillared barracks on the right faced the Hospital and Sergeant's Quarters, with Headquarters (where Mother's office was) in the center.

wonderful years as caretakers, but was eventually transferred to Fort Heath in Winthrop, Massachusetts for a very short stay. Then they went back to Corregidor in the Philippine Islands.

There were three other caretakers: two unmarried privates and Corporal Barney Kirkland. Corporate Kirkland was a southern gentleman who was very gallant, quiet, and diplomatic. His wife, Agnes or "Aylie," also of Irish background, came from South Boston and did not much care for "pollocks." She was the direct opposite of her husband. If opposites attract, they were certainly attracted. She frequently made faux pas that poor Barney had to apologize for. Despite these, we all enjoyed a close friendship and had many good times together.

Fire!

A lthough Fort Andrews was no longer an active duty base, there were still signs reminiscent of the early days of summer picnics and parties. In the early 1930's, the Massachusetts Bay Yacht Club Association continued the tradition of summer island picnics. The bay in front of the parade grounds would be filled with boats — big boats, small boats, and those in between. Most of them were decorated with colorful flags, which were bright against their fresh clean paint. There would be music and singing. People were only just beginning to recover from the worst two years of the depression. They did not have much, but they enjoyed and appreciated what they did have. The picnics were not the blowouts that S. S. Pierce had thrown in the early 20s, but they were certainly bang-up parties. The parties always ended with the Coast Guard and the Harbor Police coming to assist the caretakers in subduing some disorderly people.

During this time Dad was working on the 16-inch gun installation at Fort Duvall on Hog Island, now called Spinnaker Island in the Harbor. Eddie, not yet in school, went to "work" daily with Dad who provided our boat, the *Tub*, as transportation carrying all the engineers from Pemberton to Duvall. They had worked since early spring and the guns would be ready to fire in September. When they were fired, some of the

Dad would bring Eddie along as he ferried engineers over to Fort Duvall on Hog Island, during the installation of the 16-inch guns pre-WWII.

windows were known to have shattered all the way over in the Town of Hull.

Once September, 1934 rolled around, we had spent a good part of the summer beautifying our house on the Island. Father and my brothers had painted inside and out. I had redecorated my room, and was pleased with the results. My girlfriend, Louise Madden, from Brookline was visiting for a few days before our senior year of school began. We were trying to make the most of the last days of our vacation with swimming, sunbathing, rowing, and fishing before returning to Brookline for the fall. Mom, Stan, and I would spend November till March in Brookline, while Dad and Eddie would remain on Peddock's. We, of course, would look forward to the Army boat allowing us to spend two days on the weekend with Dad and Ed at our real home.

I remember the day so clearly in that year of 1934. We had awakened to a beautiful September morning. There was not a ripple on the water. The sun was bright, and it was comfortably warm and a great day for fishing. We jumped into the dory with our fishing lines and bait, rowed out a few yards and dropped anchor. Mother would call us when lunch was ready. The flounder were biting, and we were chatting about taking the ferry to Hull that afternoon. Suddenly, from the shore we heard Dad shouting, "Fire, fire!"

FORT ANDREWS HOUSE BURNED

Lost Before Fireboat 44 Reached Island

Fire believed to have been caused by an explosion in a kitchen range swept through the two-story wooden dwellings at Fort Andrews on Peddocks Island early this afternoon and burned it to the ground before firemen, aboard Fireboat 44, arrived.

Alec Cees, a retired soldier and his family, including two children, occupied the house. They fled from the house and escaped injury.

When word of the fire reached Fort Banks, headquarters of the Boston Harbor fortifications, Capt M. B. Gibson, acting commander, dispatched a dozen soldiers in charge of Lieut William M. Cline to the island aboard a Government boat.

They arrived shortly after the fireboat. Heavy water lines were run from the fireboat to the building, but it was too far gone to save, and with its contents, was destroyed. Damage was estimated at $2500.

Fort Andrews, practically abandoned, is in charge of Sergt Clark, a caretaker.

September 6, 1934 article about the fire.

Looking toward the beach, I saw the back of our house ablaze. How I pulled the anchor up and rowed ashore, I will never know. Forgetting my friend and the boat, I frantically ran up the beach crying, praying, not knowing what to do, but wanting to do something, anything, to stop this horrible thing that was happening! People were running from the civilian side carrying brooms, buckets, mops, and anything else that might help extinguish the blaze. I ran to my mother who was inconsolable. Three people were comforting her and persuading her that it was impossible to go into the house to try to save the things she valued and had worked so hard to obtain. Dad, with a look of despair and disbelief, was playing the garden hose on the end of the fire he could get close to. The fire was so hot that getting very close was impossible. There was nothing anyone could do with a garden hose except let the fire burn.

When only the burning frame was left, a detachment arrived from Fort Banks (Winthrop, MA), which was about an hour away by boat. They dragged a fire hose across the hill from a hydrant on the Post and played a heavy stream of water on the boat shed. The roof of the shed was smoking and scorching and the steady stream of water turned into steam. The window glass was molten and resembled miniature waterfalls. Next door, Fred Perry and his family were moving all of their possessions out of their house. If the shed went, it would be very difficult to save their house. The hill was burning and soldiers were beating out the flames with wet brooms. All of the small pines that had been planted by the Civilian Conservation Corps. were burned to a crisp.

We were a completely demoralized family. The home we loved so much as well as most of our worldly goods were gone. All of our clothes, even Dad's newly cashed Army paycheck, which was in his suit pocket was burned, as were my friend, Louise's clothes and her diamond ring. Dad's much prized and beloved Colt revolver was destroyed. My brother Stanley, with tears in his eyes, came and put his arm around me. Eddie joined us and we three tried to console one another. Stanley said, "Everything is gone. All I could save was Mom's living room table and settee." That was all we had left. We watched almost in fascination, finding the whole thing so hard to comprehend.

By the time the firemen from the Boston Fire Boat arrived, it was far too late. Their pumper boat was docked at the Andrews' pier, which was on the other side of the island from our house. Even if they had arrived on time, their boat would be too far away from the fire. After several hours, all but a few soldiers were left. Those who remained kept wetting down the area. We discovered later that the fire started from the kerosene stove exploding. By the time the fire had smoldered, the Perrys had returned their furniture and personal property to their house. They then invited our devastated family in for food and tea. It was very comforting, but no one had much enthusiasm or desire to eat. Meanwhile, the Commanding Officer at Fort Banks ordered the hospital steward's quarters at Fort Andrews be opened for us. A boat arrived with beds, blankets, pots, pans, china, and food. Also by order of the Commanding Officer, we were to remain in these quarters for a couple of months, or until such time as we were reoriented.

The Andrews' caretaker at the time, Sergeant Clark and his wife and the other caretakers were very concerned and extremely helpful. They made sure we had lights and water, and that everything the Army sent was set up and useful. They invited us to dinner until we could manage on our own. In the ensuing days, heartbroken, Dad, Stan and young Eddie cleared away some of the debris. The Army let Dad use the materials from the two wooden Army buildings on the inner Post—the old carpenter shop and the plumbing shop—that was being torn down, to rebuild our house. Stanley and an off duty soldier would transport the lumber from the inner Post to our area with the caretaker's old Ford truck. Later in the fall, Dad had a tool shed built that he would live in while he set the foundation for the new house. He laid the foundation with granite and brick set in the ground with a twelve by twelve wooden sill. He planned to continue in the spring. A new house, however, was not in the cards for several moons.

In the summer of 1935, the Quinns were stationed in Vermont, so we rented their cottage until such time as they would return or we had a place to live. There were still building materials to move. Stan and two young soldiers continued to make trip after trip bumping over the rough rutted hill road in that old Ford truck. They unloaded and stacked windows, doors, planks, siding, a tub, all kinds of fixtures, hardware, and slate for a roof. Mother commuted back and forth from Brookline to make sure everything was running smoothly there.

When Mother was away, I did the cooking with occasional help from Eddie during that summer. He made delicious muffins from scratch since there were few mixes in those days. Stan did not care much for cooking, but he policed the area and it would sparkle. Eddie liked to cook (another sign of his later career choice as a chemist) so we balanced our chores and it worked out very well. Dad always prepared breakfast and always made his mashed potatoes for dinner. Quite a bit was accomplished that summer, but the house had only a skeletal start. We spent the winter in Brookline and it passed slowly.

Our poor house that lay in rubble that late summer day of 1934.

Stan was a student at Northeastern University, Eddie was in grammar school, and I was studying dance at The Boston Conservatory of Music. Mother was working as a dressmaker and Dad kept the home fires burning.

Finally, June 1936 was at hand, which meant another summer on Peddock's. All of us were anxious to get going. Once we settled into island life again, a week had passed when our water supply was suddenly nonexistent. Of course, difficulty was no stranger to us. Island living seemed to invite it. Even though we had taken our water supply more or less for granted, now we had to scramble for it.

Everyone on the Post was waterless because a ship anchored in the western part of Hull Gut had severed our pipeline when it had lifted its anchor. We needed water now, and the old Portuguese-built well on the civilian side had been filled in. We weren't going to be able to wait to see when and if it could be reopened. Our little boat, the *Tub*, became our water supply ferry. It seemed as though we carried enough water

Our little boat The Tub *(here with Eddie) came through in many ways for us and the other islanders: from transporting engineers to the gun installation on Fort Duvall to carrying water from the mainland after the water main was broken.*

from Hull to fill the Harbor that summer. Three times a week, Dad and my brothers carried several GI trashcans full of fresh water each trip.

Barrels caught rainwater for washing, and we flushed the toilet with seawater carried up from the beach by the bucketful. It was two months before the repairs on the pipeline were made and everyone could go back to taking a bath!

Not having our old house presented a different life predicament. Our house was still not completed when the Quinns had returned from Vermont to the Island in 1937. So, we had to think of something. Dad and the boys moved the old iron boat out of the big shed and made the shed their sleeping quarters. The smaller shed was turned into a kitchen and bedroom for Mother, and we painted it white and added new floor covering, got a small table, and a cook stove which actually was a galley stove from a boat. Dad built a wall cabinet for dishes, and other things. It was rather cramped, but functional at that time.

Before the pipe broke, this is what my family's water bill looked like for the summer of 1933.

We had no water piped into the house or our new living quarters in the sheds, at this time. The outdoors was used to advantage since we did our laundry outside in a big Army galvanized wash tub and scrubbed on a washboard. We used the same outdoor method for washing our dishes and vegetables. The ocean proved a cold bath (the Harbor water was clean then), and the hose provided fresh water with which to rinse off. I quickly adopted a spit bath technique. I bathed in a huge Navy dishpan retrieved from the ocean. The Navy had discarded it when they were at anchor in the channel in front of our house. We enjoyed the luxury of warm water, which I heated on the wood stove. Our only modern conveniences were a flush toilet at the far end of the big shed and electricity. My brothers and I did not mind roughing it camp style, but my parents were less than enthusiastic, especially after having a comfortable home with all the conveniences.

Dad was not feeling too well. He was troubled with arthritis and his eyes were bothering him. It was diagnosed as glaucoma. In those days it was incurable and blindness would result. He stayed on the Island for shorter periods of time, so Mother would commute to Brookline as we had Army boat service.

Finally, after working very hard to collect building materials for the house and the foundation, we had finally rebuilt our once treasured home, including the toilet and shower. We were able, once again, to take our walks along the beach.

Marriage and Change

In the late 1930s, I had graduated from high school and entered the Boston Conservatory for Dance just around the same time that Europe was embroiled in World War II. I had a group of friends and we all went out together, including my future husband, Buddy Silvia. I hadn't paid much attention to Buddy, until the Christmas of 1937, at one of our mutual friends' party. He had presented me with a bottle of lovely perfume, and I had absolutely nothing for him. It came to me as a great surprise, since my friend was trying to set me up with someone else. So, when I received this gift, I ran out of the party, and bought some handkerchiefs and boxed them up. When I returned to the party, I handed him my gift and said, "This is so you don't have to use your sleeve." Within the following year, I moved to New York City to dance professionally, and Bud followed me with a degree in architecture from the Beaux Art School, and a job at a Manhattan firm. On December 11, 1938, we exchanged vows in a civil ceremony at City Hall.

Living in New York never deterred me from visiting Peddock's. I made certain that my dancing career allowed me to be on the Island from May to November, and my new husband, well, he would visit on the weekends. When I would return to the Island in the late 1930s, Boston Harbor had maintained its shipping industry but the forts were inactive. We continued

The newlyweds:
Mr. and Mrs. Buddy Silvia

our daily walks and boat rides throughout the Harbor Islands, and began to notice some definite changes to the coastline.

We frequently found discarded items from ships or Navy vessels. In 1938, a freighter called the *City of Salisbury* ran aground on Graves Light shoals and sank. From its holds came drums of coconut oil, and one of the drums washed up on our beach. Eddie, who many years later became a chemist, made coconut oil soap and shampoo which lasted us for years and years. Other times, huge casks of real tea washed up on the beach. However, by the time we got some of it, the sea had pretty well soaked through the casks so the tea was mostly unpalatable. There were also huge bales of natural rubber, but no one knew what to do with them. It was said that someone once found tigers that had been shipped to the zoo but drowned below decks, but there was no proof to substantiate that rumor.

Boats docked in South Boston circa late 1930s.

The Army Base in South Boston had many other interesting cargo ships loading and unloading all sorts of goods such as
wool, lumber, exotic oils, hides, and coal. There were great
numbers of Japanese ships loading scrap iron from hopper cars
with big cranes and tremendous dome-shaped magnets. The
noise was thunderous as tons of scrap fell into the bowels of
the ships. Many of these foreign ships would have to stop
on Gallops Island, and sometimes would be quarantined. The
father of one of my classmates living on Gallops was the head
doctor who would board the foreign ships in the outer harbor.
Dr. Sweeney inspected everyone on board for disease. If the
ship was OK, it was passed into port. If there was a communi-
cable disease on board, the boat was quarantined and kept in
the outer harbor with a yellow quarantine flag flying as a warning to keep away. If hospitalization was needed, Gallops Island
had a hospital, doctors, nurses, and quarantine quarters. There
were several quarantine boats scurrying in and out of the harbor

daily since there was such a great deal of shipping in the Port of Boston throughout the 1920's, '30's and '40's.

Besides the flotsam and jetsam that washed up on shore from the harbor traffic, changes in the contour of the land became more evident even in the late 1930s. It wasn't difficult to become aware of the soil and placement changes of rock and erosion on the beach and hill banks. I remember when I was a little girl in the very early 1920's, we used to walk a path on the rim of the hill about twenty-five or thirty feet in from the outer edge of the bank. Right in the middle of the path was a pudding stone about one-and-a-half feet in diameter, which we had walked on as part of the path. Gradually, as the bank eroded, it had moved. Now, after these many years, the gigantic stone was completely out of the bank on the hillside and exposed down on the beach.

When Fort Andrews had been an active military base during World War I, the Army had to find ways of disposing certain materials. Often, they would bury unwanted material— such as paint, metals, oils, or chemicals and anything that could not be incinerated had to be buried. In those days, this was seen as a safe disposal method. At times, this proved wrong. For instance, one time when we were little, our neighbor Don Hall was scavenging the beach and brought home some iron cylinders that seemed perfect for a six year old child to build log type cabins, block houses, or use to decorate the edge of the walk. They looked like ordinary harmless window weights so he piled them in the yard. Don played with them as a kid, but as he grew older they were left in a pile and eventually discarded. Some years later on a late summer afternoon, just north of our row of houses where we could not see, the hill was in a blaze of fire. It brought villagers who saw smoke and fire from their section of the Island, running with buckets, brooms, shovels and anything else they could grab to fight a fire. Sergeant Bill McCusker, our then senior caretaker, dressed

Pudding Rock was as big as a medium-sized house once it had emerged from Middle Head.

in spanking white pants—already cleaned up for chow after having taken care of Army property all day—arrived breathless and panting and without his teeth. He joined the firefighters and issued almost sergeant-like orders.

A bucket brigade was already passing buckets of seawater at a fast pace up the beach to the top of the hill. Others were trying to beat the flames out with whatever they had in hand. A strong west wind was hampering all efforts to kill the blaze. Discouraged, but persistent, they fought on, when suddenly as if by magic, the wind died and so did the flames. The fire was over. Everyone wanted to know how it had started. No one knew. About a week later we were walking the beach when we made a discovery. On checking a puff of smoke down near the low tide mark, we found what we had thought to be window weights tucked among the rocks. They were not window weights at all but phosphorous bombs! We discovered that the Army had buried the bombs in the hill near the dump after World War I. Slowly, as the hill eroded, the bombs slid down the hill into the water and eventually worked their way around the Head. In storms, the waves tossed them here and there. Some landed low in the water and others high near the grass and flotsam above the tide line on the hill. As the iron casings and phosphorous filling oxidized.... Voila, fire! After all, that was their purpose. For weeks after that fire, we hunted and collected bombs. Who knows, there may still be some around.

World War II and POWs

When the United States joined the war efforts overseas in 1941, Fort Andrews was once again called to duty. As routine as Army life is known to be, activities continued to follow a definite pattern even in wartime. The necessities of maintaining an Army post for 1,000 men was a good sized operation. Food and all categories of supplies had to be unloaded from barges and boats, reloaded on trucks and trucked to barracks, warehouses, stables, the gym, the Post Exchange (PX), and a dozen other places.

Part of a day's routine included general building maintenance, truck and machinery repair, keeping the Post in GI condition, grass cut, papers and cigarette butts removed. Along with all this activity, serious training for real war took a major part of the day and sometimes the night. Post activity generally began at six a.m. and usually continued till chow time at five p.m. After chow, if there was no training, came social activities. On Saturdays during daylight hours there might be a U.S.O. dance or, once in a while, big band entertainment. Also, sometimes there was a baseball or basketball game.

Otherwise, there were the movies. Most social activities took place in the new wooden building built where the old Company K barracks had stood before it burned down in 1926. At one end of the hall was a stage. The hall itself had many movable benches, which made it easy to accommodate almost

The 59th Co. Coast Artillery Corps. baseball team.

any activity. After dinner, most people on the Post, including the soldiers and civilians, headed for the PX, which was now in the old bakery. Bread had not been baked there for twenty years.

The PX was packed with soldiers, civilians, cigarette smoke, and jukebox music. Nat King Cole and the Mills Brothers were probably the most popular singers of the day on our Post. Their recordings of "Paper Doll" and "Mona Lisa" seemed to be played over and over. After about an hour of smoke, 3.2 beer, Coca-Cola, small talk, arguing, laughing, and music, everyone took off up the road to the Rec Hall for the movies or any other entertainment. Often after the movies, most would re-turn to the PX. Soldiers who were friends of Sam Perry would often come down to his house for coffee and a bite to eat, with perhaps a game of Rummy 500 thrown in for good measure.

We came to realize over the years that there were always surprises—and secret maneuverings—on an Army post. One such surprise came one early morning when I awoke to loud male voices outside my window. Gingerly, I lifted the shade and peeked out the narrow slit. There were trees running all over the yard. The trees turned out to be camouflaged soldiers pretending that they were a forest. The Medics were trying to hide a field hospital unit they hoped to set up.

The steep hill in back of my house was a challenge. Carrying medical instruments, huge boxes of medications and operating tables up or down this hill was no picnic. Carrying a big man on a stretcher (and they all looked big), required brute strength. It was easier to roll everything down the hill. So, needless to say, the stretcher occupants got up and walked and the boxes rolled. A working hospital was set up almost at my doorstep. Splints were applied to arms and legs and heads were bandaged. The mock patients were the butt of jokes and child's play. It was hard to realize, and a dreadful thought, that all of this battle play would soon take on the reality of a real battle-field.

The garrison was constantly changing as each group was trained and moved out usually overseas to Europe or the Pacific. The men in my life were also shipped away: my husband was stationed in Los Alamos, New Mexico, where he was on the team to design the elevator for the "Fat Boy," the atom bomb. He was even there when they tested the first one. My oldest brother, Stan, joined the navy in the South Pacific, while Eddie was with General Patten's army in charge of bomb disposal in Germany.

It was very difficult to say goodbye not only to your own family, but even to the men who you knew casually, from the PX, the dance hall, bowling or the movies. The horrible realization that they were leaving their country and going to an unknown place, perhaps to be killed or captured and maybe tortured was very sad and frightening to us. It was difficult to keep the tears back even though you barely knew some of the young men. They were all getting on boats leaving the peace and safety of the Island to go fight. Their courage and morale

Mother with Stanley in his WWII uniform.

was unbelievable. They were proud and brave, some even adventurous. Those of us who were left behind were worried and afraid. This gloomy mood lasted too long, ending only when the war turned and fewer men were being sent overseas. Some young men from the 241st remained at Fort Andrews until the caretakers took over after the war.

Fort Andrews had been garrisoned mostly by the 241st and the 9th Coast Artillery whose current base was Fort Banks at Winthrop. There was also a company or two of Medics. Many of these young medical men were volunteers from the Kentucky mountains. Some had never worn shoes before coming into the Army. Their tales of rather primitive but creative living in the hills were fascinating. In spite of the ominous specter of their way of life, they appreciated Army life and were deeply devoted to our country. Generally they were uneducated but had "smarts" and common sense. Their knowledge

*Visiting from NYC, here
I am posing with my brother,
Eddie, in uniform.*

of natural medicine and how to coexist with nature and the outdoors was extensive. That is probably why they landed in the Medical Corps. Their regard and respect for women left a great deal to be desired, but they were fast learning that Army women would not tolerate disrespect and they were making every effort to be gentlemen (at least on the Army post). When women came on the scene at the dock, the PX, the theater, or wherever a group of men gathered, the swearing and rough language became inaudible (street language was not acceptable or tolerated in mixed company at that time). There were comparatively few women on the Post so it was not a difficult task to control respect.

The hospital was staffed with two doctors and four orderlies. After all, the Army was always giving shots for something and this is where everyone lined up. There were several male patients in the hospital recuperating from wounds received in

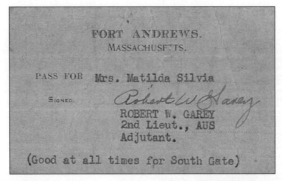

I needed a pass to get on the Island during World War II.

the Pacific Theater. Most were ambulatory and were almost ready to go back to duty or to be discharged. Several others were quarantined because they had venereal diseases and were kept away from other GIs. Apparently they did not heed any of the matchbook cover warnings to cover up before striking. We spent time at the hospital talking to the few patients, writing letters, sometimes playing cards or checkers, talking or just listening to their war escapades to help pass the time.

In the early spring before the hills put on their mantle of green, the Army would control burn the area. The soldiers were careful not to harm the wild blackberries and beach plums. Burning never seemed to hinder the growth of the wild mushrooms. When I was a child, picking these goodies was a ritual. So, in 1944, when the picking season arrived before the Army set fire to the area, Vi Perry and I—now in our late twenties—took off for the hills to the berry patches with our pails in hand.

On this particular day, Vi and I dressed in our bright yellow rain gear, that would protect us against the murderous 1/2 inch thorns of the blackberries. The blazing sun was beating down sending rivulets of perspiration dripping down our bodies all the way to our ankles beneath our plastic suits of armor. We climbed the hill near the radio shack to our favorite black-

Vi Perry and me all grown up.

berry patch where the bushes were loaded with fruit. Absorbed in picking and chatting, we were completely oblivious to the fact that we were almost imperceptibly being surrounded by men. Slightly startled, we stared at them as they tried to communicate in sign language and very broken English. We realized we were meeting head on with the Italian Prisoners of War (POWs), which scuttlebutt had told us would be arriving any day. We had been asked by the commandant to remain aloof unless we were with GIs. Rumor had it that these particular prisoners had been troublesome in the South Boston POW compound and were being sent to the Island where they would not have easy contact with civilians—particularly women. We found them to be gentlemen, but after very brief

Housing for the Italian prisoners of war.

communication, Vi and I, following orders, decided to say "good-bye" and hustle home.

The prisoners were restricted to various areas. The ridge of the hill in back of our house, beyond a short area from their barracks was one boundary. They could sit on the ridge overlooking our homes and yards and keep track of any activity going on below. It was my habit to fish a couple of times a week, sometimes with Vi and sometimes alone. After stowing my gear and bait in my boat I would shove off and row out maybe a hundred yards. It was quiet on the hill, not a sole visible on the Island. By the time I pulled in my first flounder, the ridge would be populated with POWs all watching. I usually caught enough flounder for lunch or dinner. Occasionally, if I was particularly lucky, I would catch a lobster or two. There were sharks and skates around also. When I caught them it was time to go home. I would never pull one of these monsters into my boat. I would tie them on a short line to a ring in the stern of the boat, haul my anchor and tow them ashore. By the time I hit the beach there was an Italian curiosity committee in the distance. After taking the hook out of the critters I would leave them high and dry on the beach. As soon as the POWs realized I was abandoning my catch and after I had moved away, they would come and scoop up the catch and lug them up the hill to the barracks. I was told they cooked them in olive oil and enjoyed a meal of what we considered trash fish.

Most of the Italian prisoners seemed to be happy on Andrews and appeared to be grateful to be prisoners of the Americans. The spirit of the prisoners was excellent in spite of a few years of confinement. They had escaped Mussolini's clutches and the horrors of the desert. They were very resentful of their government and Mussolini. They heaped nothing but blame, hatred, and contempt on him for joining Hitler in a senseless war. By 1940, Mussolini was practically a done deal and eventually he would pay for it.

The Italian prisoners were mostly responsible for loading combat materials to be first shipped to the Port of Embarkation (POE) at the South Boston Army Base and then onto the war zone. This type of work was heaven for them compared to what they had experienced in the hot, dirty, insect-ridden desert area of North Africa. They had access to certain areas of the Post with movies every night, a canteen with all the special goodies they wanted, and most of all freedom from the war. They did their own guard duty with an occasional check by the GIs, as well as getting paid for their work at the POE.

On weekends, they rotated on a two-day pass to Boston. One group alternated each weekend from Friday night until Sunday night. Those remaining on the Island were allowed to have friends and relatives visit them on either day of the weekend. The guests were not allowed to stay overnight. As far as I know, no one went AWOL.

Actually, we had little personal contact with the Italian prisoners. They would greet us with smiles and a salute when we met them on the Post. Those who spoke even a little English liked to converse, but few occasions arose. Their life was pretty relaxed. Some areas of the Post were out of bounds to

Post-war signs: Submarine nets warded off German submarines. The long wooden net crossed the harbor between the main land and an island.

them, including the Post Exchange (PX). One day when I was entering the PX (or the canteen) an American soldier handed me a letter from a young Italian POW named Frank. Apparently he saw me and wished to meet me. This never happened, of course.

The first time I saw a soccer game was when I watched the prisoners play. It was fast, exciting, and rough. Once in a while one of the prisoners would be carried off to the hospital. As far as I could gather, there were never any serious injuries. They were completely devoted to this game. America's favorite pastime of baseball seemed not to be of much interest to them. I was a bit surprised because they seemed to readily adopt American customs, habits, and actions. We got to know and admire one particular POW who was a doctor. He was a wonderful, kind, understanding, concerned, and fine doctor. All the Americans on the Post thought he was great. Whenever they had a medical problem they sought him out. He wanted to return to the United States after the war, but I'm not sure if he ever did.

When the war in Europe was over and the war with Japan would soon end, the POWs had practically finished their time as prisoners. Soon the men would be leaving for home and they were all happy and excited. Their belongings would be moved to the mainland for shipment to Italy.

For Sale: Peddock's Island

Now, with the war over, Fort Andrews would change dramatically. There was daily activity as the Post was being deactivated. Career soldiers from Fort Banks were replacing the draftees. A constant flow of barges and boats were removing Army material, horses, and machinery, and storing what was to be left on the Island. The Post was kept in excellent condition. A detail was left with our old time friend Bill McCusker when the bulk of the GIs left. Bill took over as boss and caretaker. We heard and were told that the General Services Administration (GSA) was taking over and that Andrews was going to be put up for auction. That took some time, but meanwhile we had other Army caretakers.

Sergeant Shoesmith and his family stayed for a couple of years as caretaker. Shoesmith, his wife and their two small girls provided good friendship, companionship, and assistance in anything we had to do. Dull moments were few and far between with the Shoesmiths. When they were transferred, we hated to see them go. They were replaced by Sergeant Bob Kohler and his family who also remained a couple of years. Sam Perry, now an island resident for over 56 years, became interim caretaker for a very short period when Andrew Sweeney joined him. Andrew had a good-sized boat and became sole caretaker of Forts Warren and Standish.

By the time the 1950's had arrived, the GSA had become

Three of my favorite men: Eddie (left), Stan (right), my husband Bud (underneath me).

"boss" and they were putting the Post up for sale at auction. The time between the Army's command of the Island, the GSA auction, and the final sale brought both curious and genuinely interested people to inspect Fort Andrews. One person to arrive was Mrs. Franklin D. Roosevelt with some representatives of Boys Town, Nebraska. It was said the government would sell the fort to them for the proverbial one dollar. The Post was in excellent condition at that time (still under Army care), and I'm told Boys Town was very impressed and interested and wanted very much to have it. However, after careful calculation and much deliberation, they decided the cost of water transportation to the Island was prohibitively expensive. They reluctantly turned it down. We had no real way to verify all the particulars, but the visit that we witnessed certainly prompted all the scuttlebutt, which we accepted.

Fort Andrews was finally sold at auction in 1953 to Isadore Bromfield, who had part ownership of East Coast Realty. Bromfield really just wanted the parcel of land next to his shipyard in East Boston. But, since Peddock's was attached to that piece of government owned land, he got us as well. We were told that he really didn't want the Island, but took it mainly to enlarge his shipyard. He paid $35,000 for Fort Andrews and the East Head's fortification, and $25,000 for the rest of the Island, which included the civilian side.

As time went on, the new owner hired several civilian caretakers to replace the Army personnel. These included Gus Williams, Mr. Atwood and Andrew Sweeney. Finally, young Eddie and Judy McDevitt took over. For about seventeen years, Isadore Bromfield was a very congenial landlord who paid fond attention to the Islanders and asked for very fair compensation in return. The Islanders paid rent for the land to Bromfield who kept our water running and the Island in good condition. Unfortunately, there were a couple of bad episodes with a company that was dredging Hull Gut and we lost our electricity when they tore up the cable. We heard Mr. Bromfield was compensated, but it was more costly to repair the cable than he thought even though he tried. Unfortunately, the electricity was never successfully replaced. However, Mr. Bromfield did reduce our rent in compensation for our loss.

Even with people evident and caretakers on the Harbor Islands, there were still unfortunate incidents with vandalism. The destruction the vandals perpetrated was vast. From the 1800's until World War II some islands in Boston Harbor were privately owned by rugged outdoor individuals who loved the ocean and the beauty and quiet away from the mainland. They were not afraid to battle the elements or to undergo the often miserable hardships that presented themselves. Julia Arthur,

Posing on Little Brewster Island with Boston Light within a few feet beside me.

the silent movie actress (*The Man of Destiny*, *Uncle Tom's Cabin*), was one of these individuals. She supposedly lived on both Calf and Middle Brewster Island. I only remember her mansion on Middle Brewster. I saw it as a rather dilapidated but recognizably once beautiful home, which changed a few years later with the assistance of some vandals. The house, which stood so regally with beautiful paneling, windows, and a magnificent staircase with the white rope, was now in shambles. China and glass were smashed, and everything was hacked to pieces. During one of my excursions, I managed to dig a lovely dish from the debris. My efforts were rewarded with an unscathed plate of Seneca China that, I assume, was from Julia Arthur's china closet. Now it is in my china closet and I treasure it.

Boston Harbor was our playground and its islands were

part of our lives. We had friends on most of the islands and sometimes went to visit them. Transportation would continue to be difficult and sometimes an all day affair. We would visit friends at Fort Warren, walk around the casemates (the underground buildings) through the sally port, inspect the moat, and have lunch with a friend who lived in one of the casemates.

When Bud would visit, we would sometimes go to Boston Light. This almost became a Saturday night ritual, weather permitting. We would jump into our boat *Skip* and run out to visit John and Libby Honors, and their small daughter, Leslie. John was a senior lighthouse keeper with the U.S Coast Guard. Dinner was part of the visit. The rocks and waters of the Brewster Islands (which included Great Brewster, Little Brewster, where Boston Light sits, Middle Brewster, Calf, Little Calf, Green, Shag Rocks, and Graves Islands) provided a perfect home for lobsters, crabs, cod and haddock, and the mud between the rocks yielded clams. Usually dinner, much to our delight, consisted of these delicacies.

We would walk the small island beach then climb the winding stairs and feel the antiquity of the oldest and first lighthouse in the United States. Often we would just sit and enjoy the view and have good conversation. Before heading back to Peddock's, we would watch *Gunsmoke* on TV, shoot the breeze for a few minutes over a cup of tea, then take off for home. And, when the Honors could leave the Light, they would come to visit us. They enjoyed the space on a big island. Their Leslie, then four years old, was the most wonderful little girl who was well behaved, sweet, bright, and outgoing. She was the only child on the Light, and had only grownups for company. We loved her so much that Bud and I named our only daughter after her.

A Sad State of
Collapse . . . But Home

P eddock's Island was never deserted after World War II by
its civilian residents, some of whom had been there for
over a half a century. Even with evacuation of the U.S. Army
and its caretakers and very limited boat service, many residents
remained year round. To some, Peddock's was their home.
They had no other place to go. There were both retired and
working lobster fishermen as well as retired Army people.

During these years, I spent Spring to Fall on the Island.
Bud would visit on weekends. The Island was always a part of
my life, one I was never willing to give up, even for work, or
marriage, I suppose.

Peddock's had been at the center of our lives, and anyone
else who had grown up there. As children we embraced natural
learning and survival, and as adults, we relied on community
and simplicity. When you're raised on an island, it is difficult
to know or want any other kind of life. From never giving up
on the final catch of the day to trusting that a captain would
make it through the ice to pick you up after school. From
watching cannons explode on the hillside behind your home
to smelling the first batch of fresh bread in the Fort's bakery.
All of these experiences and memories brought you back to
The Rock, that one place that you could count on where the

Just me, waiting for the ferry on the Ft. Andrews dock.

would lull you to bed, and the neighbors would welcome you with a game of cards or a warm meal. It was very hard to imagine living for very long anywhere else. What drew you back were the people who surrounded you like the Perry families, and the storms that engulfed you. When all you could hear was the water lapping, and the waves crashing, that was when you knew you were home. This sentiment had and would pour throughout prior and future generations. This I would discover in the late 50s.

In 1957 during a routine physical, I was told by my doctor in New York that I had a tumor in my stomach that was cancerous and had to be removed immediately. I immediately informed the doctor that I would have it removed at the end of the summer after I returned from one last good summer on The Rock.

Leslie and I walking along the overgrown parade grounds of Fort Andrews, beside the enlisted men's barracks.

Halfway through what I believed to be my final summer on Peddock's, I went to a Boston doctor, who informed me that it wasn't cancer at all, but that I was with child. At age forty, that never entered my mind. Indeed, on December 11, 1958, my daughter Leslie was born. And, her first boat ride to Peddock's occurred four months later.

Leslie, Bud and I spent many years coming and going from New York to Boston Harbor and saw the Island through many changes and "squirmishes." Isadore Bromfield continued as our landlord for seventeen years, until it became eminent domain in 1970. The Metropolitan District Commission (MDC) bought it for $192,000 from the estates of Isidore Bromfield and Richard Robie, co-owners of East Coast Realty. Through

The Commanding Officer's quarters is just one of the many fortifications that is now unsafe to explore.

the late 70's, East Coast Realty sued the MDC for undervaluing the Island and settled thirteen years later in 1983 for $3.2 million.

There were many plans over the years from different Metropolitan District Commissioners, but none as of yet that has come into fruition. There have been a few building studies, but with budget cuts and island vandalism, the fort buildings have become dilapidated and unsafe to even explore. The hills that used to be control burned by the army were now overgrown. A forest now overshadows the once bold fortifications, and there is no longer water or electricity flowing onto the Island. Boston Harbor visitors are welcome to hike and picnic on the Island, but will find the fort buildings like the old PX and Officer's Quarters much too unstable. Some of the old caretakers still take their morning strolls along the beaches doing what they can to pick up some of the jetsam or pollution that floated onto the shores from the night before. But for now, Peddock's slowly erodes into the Harbor that once protected it from German subs, and quarantined fleets.

Some of the Peddock's clan gather in front of the Guard House, where my father's original house stood in 1910 (left to right): Mary Perry, Leslie, Caretaker Atwood, Lil "Nana" Perry, Me, and Fred Perry.

Due to lack of upkeep, it was quite evident that Fort Andrews and its buildings would become in such a bad state of collapse that even an uneducated surveyor would suggest the complete demolition of most of the Post. Although the MDC has had many plans for rehabilitation of the Island to another time in history, or as an ecotourism site, the Island has become its own living ghost and memories of days of yore.

For our family, and others who lived on the Island for an entire century, and saw the changes that it went through, it was difficult to express the love, interest, and complete sense of responsibility we long time island residents felt for the "Old

Soldiers on the Fort Andrews dock playing Taps.

Rock." One or even two caretakers never seemed to be adequate enough to care for the 188 acres of Peddock's, and ward off vandals or careless day trippers on motor boats.

But as the saying goes, time does march on! So, today if you wend your way down to Pemberton and look across Hull Gut, listen very carefully. Perhaps on the wind you can hear the echo of long ago commands issued through the years of drills or listen for the voices of those who lived on the Island and those who trained to proudly serve our country in her hours of need. Listen for the laughter of the day-trippers who had fun at picnics on the Island, or the whistles and sounds of the boats that traveled back and forth to the Island in all types of weather.

There is still the faint sounds of artillery in the breeze as the men long ago practiced their marksmanship; the rattle of equipage on the horses and mules as they drew the caissons;

the sound of the bugle calls for various activities; our grand flag as she would ripple on the wind and would be lowered at the end of a busy day. Also listen and you might hear the mournful sound of "Taps" as the bugler announces the end of the day and night settles over Peddock's Island and a once magnificent Fort Andrews. For all of these memories, we give thanks.

Postscript

Peddock's Island has always been of special interest to those of us who grew up near Boston's South Shore. When I was young, you knew everyone, since towns such as Scituate, Hull, Hingham and Cohasset were small. So, it was not surprising at all that Matilda Silvia knew my late husband and all of his siblings, with whom she had attended grammar school in Hull.

Like Mrs. Silvia, I grew up with a father who was a veteran of the wars, so we all knew, at a very young age, the important role the Coast Artillery Corps on Fort Andrews played in protecting our Harbors. These men kept the south shore and Boston Harbor secure in times of conflict, as well as during times of peace. From the Revolutionary to the two World Wars, soldiers, retirees and non-enlisted men patrolled the harbors, channels, and up and down the coastline keeping an eye out for U-boats and other threats.

Mrs. Silvia first contacted me in the late 1980s—along with many other families who lived out on Peddock's—regarding the Metropolitan District Commission's (MDC's) plan to tear down their homes. The MDC had claimed the island by eminent domain in 1970 that changed it from private to public land. After land surveys and research, the MDC questioned the existence of private use of the land and how the residential properties might affect the ecological issue of the Island and Boston Harbor.

With the clean up of Boston Harbor in process, disposal of sewerage would remain a concern throughout the islands. The MDC commissioner, at the time, worried about the environmental violations and hazardous risks that the sewerage and the propane tanks used for heating posed. As commissioners came and went, the vision for how the islands would be used was debated. But, the thought of the removal of families and destruction of their homes was a huge concern. Both year round and summer residents would be affected. These residents, like the Silvia family, had ancestors who made Peddock's home since the 1800s—some of them living there through the harsh winters, and creating income from the Harbor fisheries. It was beyond their wildest imaginations, that they would be asked to leave, let alone not be able to visit during the summer months.

When Mrs. Silvia called me to tell me about this, I sent my aide, Stephanie Landry, a Hull resident, to attend all the meetings regarding the issue. I understood where the MDC was coming from, but there had to be another solution to displacing these residents. I got involved and fought for these families. My suggestion all along to the MDC was that the present owners (whose names were on the permit of their homes) could live out their time at their homes, but not be allowed to pass them onto other family members. Because of the way the Andrews' estate had been set up, the residents had owned their homes under their own names, but paid rent for the land. Now that the land was publicly owned, their rights were limited. Once the original owners were no longer able to pass on their property to their heirs, the MDC would then be able to take ownership. Several years went by and the Commission accepted my suggestion.

This was a very turbulent time for the Islanders, and many residents had to give up ownership of their family homes that they too cherished visiting in the summers, or on warm days during the year. Matilda's daughter, Leslie, was one of these people affected by the ruling. Their precious home that survived the floating of 1910, and was resurrected after their house caught fire in 1934, was being abandoned for the very last time. There are some homeowners that still inhabit the Island, who have not passed the generation mark: about a half dozen year round residents, and a few dozen summer residents.

With MDC commissioners having come and gone, and the funding for the varying plans not being available, it is still unknown as to what will happen to the Harbor Islands. At times, the MDC suggests that all the residents may return to Peddock's. At other times, there are visions of transforming the Island into an ecotourism or historical preservation site. While plans change, many non-profit groups and private citizens continue to work hard to preserve the historical and environmental value that all of the islands provide.

For now, Mrs. Silvia has given us, with new and invaluable photographs, an anecdotal history of these New England treasures. After reading this memoir, those who know Peddock's well, and those who have never heard of the island will embrace the uniqueness of growing up on an island, and will want to come to explore its natural beauty and the remains of its military history.

MARY JEANETTE MURRAY
Former State Representative
Southeastern Massachusetts

Appendix A:
Military Forts

(referred to in the book)

Fort Adams, Newport, Rhode Island

Fort Banks, Winthrop, Massachusetts

Fort Devens, Ayer, Massachusetts

Fort Duvall, Hog (Spinnaker) Island, Boston Harbor

Fort Ethan Allen, Vermont

Fort Heath, Winthrop, Massachusetts

Fort Independence, Castle Island, Boston Harbor

Fort Revere, Hull, Massachusetts

Fort Standish, Lovell's Island, Boston Harbor

Fort Strong, Long Island, Boston Harbor

Fort Warren, George's Island, Boston Harbor

Appendix B:
Illustration Credits

MAP CREDITS

(Cover) Boston Bay, *Adapted and reproduced by permission of University of New Hampshire/United States Geodetic Survey map collection, 1910*

(page 4) Peddock's Island, *Adapted and reproduced by permission of University of New Hampshire/United States Geodetic Survey map collection, from map of Boston Bay, 1910*

(93) Hull, Massachusetts, *Adapted and reproduced from UNH/USGS map collection of Nantasket, 1941 and Hull, 1946*

PICTURE CREDITS

All photographs courtesy of the author and her family's collection except for the following contributors:

(page 6) Pyramidal Tents, *Koester, The Picture Man, 100 Otis Street, East Milton, MA, July 25, 1910*

(17) *Boston Traveler* Article, *September 10, 1910*

(45) Parade Grounds, *Joseph Hurney, photographer, Alfred K. Schroeder Collection, Metropolitan District Commission (MDC)*

(59) Climbing Roses with Dad, *John Paul Silk, Official photographer, United States Army*

(61) Commanding Officer's Quarters, *A. K. Schroeder Collection, MDC*

(65) Middle Head, *Alfred K. Schroeder, photographer, A. K. Schroeder Collection, MDC*

(78) *Boston Traveler* Article, *January 29, 1927, courtesy of the Boston Public Library*

(79) Boat in Ice Cakes, *A. K. Schroeder Collection, MDC*

(86) Commanding Officer Naylor, *John Paul Silk, Official photographer, United States Army*

(88) South Boston Army Base, *John Paul Silk, Official photographer, United States Army*

(92) The *Nantasket, Hull Lifesaving Museum Collection*

(94) Pemberton Hotel, *Hull Lifesaving Museum Collection*

(101) Houses on Middle Head, *Alfred K. Schroeder, photographer, A.K. Schroeder Collection, MDC*

(102) The *Bachelder, Joseph Hurney, photographer, A. K. Schroeder Collection, MDC*

(116) Christmas in Mess Hall, *Koester, The Picture Man, 100 Otis Street, East Milton, MA*

(119) Charles Lindbergh, *John Paul Silk, Official photographer, United States Army*

(119) Mrs. Lindbergh, *John Paul Silk, Official photographer, United States Army*

(121) Plane over Fort Independence (Castle Island), *A. K. Schroeder Collection, MDC*

(124) *Boston Globe* Article, *September 24, 1928*

(130) *Boston Globe* Article, *September 6, 1934*

(139) Boats at South Boston Dock, *John Paul Silk, Official photographer, United States Army*

(152) Submarine Nets, *A. K. Schroeder Collection, MDC*

(164) Bugler playing *Taps, Koester, The Picture Man, 100 Otis Street, East Milton, MA*